# ARE YOU SITTING COMFORTABLY?

## A SCATOLOGICAL SCRAPBOOK OF **SH**... AND ALL ABOUT **IT**

SUSAN STRANKS & DON GRANT

Inter faeces et urinam nascimur.
*(We are born between shit and piss.)*
St Odon of Cluny.

MACDONALD
Macdonald Futura Publishers
London

First published in 1980 in Great Britain by
Macdonald · London and Sydney
Macdonald Futura Publishers
Paulton House
8 Shepherdess Walk
London N1 7LW

ISBN 0 354 04580 6

Printed in Great Britain by Purnell & Sons Ltd
Paulton (Bristol) and London

**This book is dedicated to**
**CLOACINA**
**Goddess of the common sewer**
**CREPITUS**
**God of conveniences**
**STERCUTIUS**
**God of ordure**

Do ye not yet understand that whatsoever entereth in at the mouth goeth into the belly and is cast out into the draught?

*Matthew XV,* 17.

# Acknowledgements

We would like to thank the following for permission to quote:

Jonathan Cape Ltd. for *Portnoy's Complaint* by Philip Roth, *Ending Up* by Kingsley Amis, *Somerset Maugham* by Ted Morgan, and Adrian Mitchell's 'Famous Weak Bladder Blues' from *Out Loud* (Cape Goliard Press); A.D. Peters and Co. Ltd. for *The Sun King* by Nancy Mitford (Hamish Hamilton Ltd.), *Men at Arms* by Evelyn Waugh (Chapman and Hall Ltd.), *Unreliable Memoirs* by Clive James (Jonathan Cape Ltd.); David Higham Associates Ltd. for *Staying On* by Paul Scott (Heinemann), *The Smallest Room* by John Pudney (Michael Joseph), *The Victorian Chaise Longue* by Marghanita Laski (The Cresset Press); George Allen and Unwin (Publishers) Ltd. for *Cleanliness and Godliness* by Reginald Reynolds; Robert Hale Ltd. for *The Witches' Gospel* by Charles Bowness; A.P. Watt Ltd. for *Man's Presumptuous Brain* by A.T.W. Simeons (Longmans Green and Co. Ltd.; Rodale Press for *Encyclopaedia of Common Diseases* (available from the publishers); The Bodley Head for *All Quiet on the Western Front* by Erich Maria Remarque (Putnam and Co. Ltd.); Satellite Books for *Witch Amongst Us* by Lois Bourne; Hodder and Stoughton Ltd. for *The Rise and Fall of the British Nanny* by Jonathan Gathorne-Hardy; William Kimber for *Napoleon's Death: An Inquest* by Frank Richardson; Michael Joseph for *The Shell Book of Firsts* by Patrick Robertson; Harvard University Press for *The Healing Hand* by Guido Majno; Arlington Books for *The Penny Spenders* by George Houghton; Cassells for *Coprophilia: A Peck of Dirt* by Terence McLaughlin; Thorsons for *A Romany Guide to Health*; The Permanent Press for *Private Moments in Public Places*; Weidenfeld and Nicolson for Anthony Storr's piece in *The World of the Public School*, edited by George Macdonald Fraser; Macmillan for *Mozart's Letters to His Family* translated by Emily Anderson; Sigmund Freud Copyrights Ltd, the Institute of Psycho-Analysis and the Hogarth Press Ltd for *New Introductory Lectures* in Volume 22 of *The Standard Edition of the Complete Psychological Works of Sigmund Freud* translated and edited by James Strachey; Routledge and Kegan Paul for *Clean and Decent* by L. Wright.

Our special thanks to the following:
Reginald Williams at the Department of Prints and Drawings, British Museum, for supplying the Rembrandt, Gilray and Hogarth prints so speedily; The Victoria and Albert Museum for permission to use the Beardsley drawings; Ralph Steadman for the use of his 'du Maurier' pastiche; The British Science Museum for historical notes and photograph of Bramah's Water Closet; Sybil Welsh for helping us dig out the hard bits at the London Library; Bowater-Scott Corporation Ltd. for historical notes and early toilet-paper advertisements; the staff of the Chelsea and Kensington, Wandsworth Borough, Richmond Borough and Marylebone Borough libraries for being anything but po-faced; Jonathan Adams, Richard Baker, George Butler, John Cleese, Jilly Cooper, Kenny Everett, Eba, Simone and Gregor Grant, Belle Heaphy, Anthony Jay, Peter Land, Tom Lehrer, Mrs Morgan at BMA House, Eddy Puma, Andrew and Robin Ray, Dr Michael Scott, William Simons, Bertha Woodward, Hugh Whitemore and Peter Wolfe for their kindness and help in compiling this book and for not being *deterred* by the subject matter. Also to Richard Johnson, our editor, for smiling throughout, and to Anne Davison, who in spite of being up to her eyes in it, managed to wade through without making waves.

We also found the following sources useful:
*The Good Loo Guide* by Jonathan Routh, *Temples of Convenience* by Lucinda Lampton, *The Lost Rivers of London* by Nicholas Barton, *A Certain World: A Commonplace Book* by W.H. Auden, *End Product (The First Taboo)* by Dan Sabbath and Mandel Hall, *Dict. of Historical Slang* edited by Eric Partridge, *No Laughing Matter: The Rationale of the Dirty Joke* by George Legman, *The British Medical Journal*, *The Water Closet* by Roy Palmer, *Costumes for Births, Marriages and Deaths* by Phyllis Cunnington and Katherine Lucas, *A Pocketful of Ribaldry* edited by Alec Brown, *Mrs Grundy: Studies in English Prudery* by Peter Fryer, *Flushed With Pride: The Story of Thomas Crapper* by Wallace Reyburn, *Management of Constipation* edited by Sir Francis Avery Jones and Edmund W. Godding, and *Which? Magazine*.

# PREFAECES

Compiling this album could have been a pain in the ass. There is not much (open) demand for the kind of material it contains, and, had it not been for the patient good humour of countless librarians (whoever said they were stuffy?) we might not have been '. . . sitting comfortably' now. Many of the choice bits lie hidden discreetly under SOCIAL HISTORY, PSYCHOLOGY, TROPICAL MEDICINE and other such broad categories; *The Penny Spenders*, George Houghton's hilarious but poignant account of his prostate troubles (now sadly out of print), was discovered for instance in Marylebone's medical library between two vast and learned tomes on urinology . . . and we took ages winkling out an apt authoritative note on Napoleon's piles.

Thanks to the giggling encouragement of the aforementioned guardians of the print, and to the good orifices of so many eager to tell their own tales of woe along with other dreadful anecdotes, we have ended up with an overflowing heap of the stuff. So what to leave out? Tears have flowed for the many extracts, from James Joyce's *Ulysses* to Billy Connolly's 'Thoughts on Public Urinals', which couldn't be squashed in (Macdonald Phewtura ran out of paper). There was a fight about Kingsley Amis's thought-nudging poem *Shitty* which I lost, on the grounds that it wasn't shitty enough. We had to drop a lovely bit of Eliot (T.S.) and a passionate monologue from John Osborne's play *Luther* because their publishers felt this book was not a suitable setting for them. There is so much more, far beneath the scope of this small publication, still to be plumbed – we have only skimmed the surface.

While doing so, for my part, I learned to say 'turd' and 'shit' without having first to be angry and have read a great deal more good literature than before, which must go to show that ten million flies can't all be wrong.

*Susan Stranks*

I feel eminently qualified to do a book of this nature as I have been every day of my life – and sometimes twice.

Don Grant

When Adam and Eve were young
And paper wasn't invented
You wiped your arse
On a blade of grass
And went away contented

# BETWEEN TWO STOOLS

## (A POTTED HISTORY)

*Once upon a time there was a hole in the ground and, beneath, a fast-flowing stream. 'Eureka!' Water-borne sanitation!*

It didn't take long for man to discover that if he defecated around his own camp-fire, pretty soon he had to move camp. So he took himself for a short walk each day, and deposited his waste where it would be washed away by the rains or dried up by the sun – in which case it became handy for fuel or building material.

What about the towns? The two earliest known domestic privies survive in India at Mohenjo-Daro (3250–2750 BC). Surprisingly they are connected to drainage gullies through outlets in the walls, and would probably have been regularly sluiced with water. Six others remain at the Palace of Sargon, the Sumerian King (2350 BC). There is a classic example in Ancient Egypt at Tel-el-Armana (1370–1350 BC), and a beauty at the Palace of Knossos. Lawrence Wright in his book *Clean and Decent* says: 'The Knossos latrines are remarkably "modern". One of these, on the ground floor, evidently had a wooden seat, and may have had an earthenware pan like a modern "wash-out" closet, as well as a reservoir for flushing-water. Save for one short-lived water-closet of Elizabethan times, England had nothing comparable with this until the eighteenth century. The Queen's apartments, with a private stair-case leading to a secluded "withdrawing room" and bedrooms above, a bathroom adjoining, and a short passage leading to a "toilette chamber", had "all modern conveniences" carefully planned and scientifically worked out. Two enclosed light-wells ensured fresh air and a diffused reflected light.'

Where there's muck there's brass, but it took Emperor Titus Flavius Vespasian to cash in on the fact that 'necessity knows no laws' by establishing the first pay-toilets in Rome, known as *latrinae* or *stercorariae*. He was also reputed to sell the urine to dye-makers, the profit from which was used for public expenditure, i.e. to build more urinals. When criticized he would reply, '*Pecunia non olet*' (money does not stink). However, the French '*urinoirs*', known until recently as '*Vespasiennes*', afforded no such charge for their use.

As Rome declined and fell so did the quality and number of available latrines and, in Europe at any rate, it took hundreds of disease-ridden 'midden-years' before we got it together again.

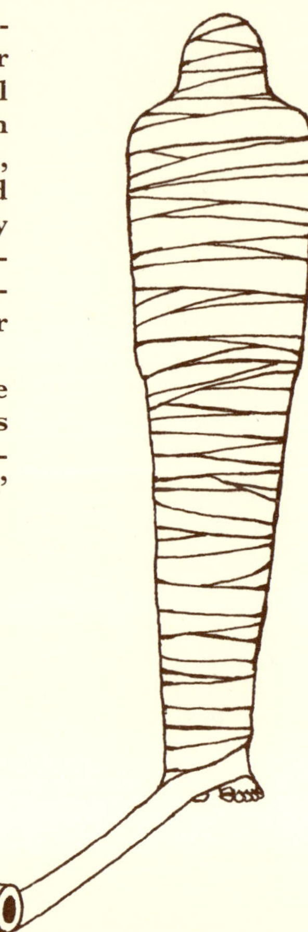

Garde-robes were the best toilet accommodation any medieval castle could offer. With luck, there was one on each floor with a seat made of wood or stone, perched over an open hole through which your contribution tumbled, its slimy trail following all the others down the outside wall to the moat below. The name 'garde-robe' came from the fact that winter robes and furs were stored there through the summer months in the belief that the draughts kept moths away; no doubt the smell offended them as well.

*'Cloak-room' is similarly used today to indicate lavatory facilities.*

*Harington's water-closet.*

SIR JOHN HARINGTON, godson to Queen Elizabeth I, invented the first known valve closet in 1589. His *FANTASTICAL TREATISE (A NEW DISCOURSE ON A STALE SUBJECT)* called the *METAMORPHOSIS OF AJAX* was written in 1596 and included this poem.

A godly father sitting on a draught,
To do as neede, and nature hath us taught;
Mumbled (as was his maner) certen prayr's,
And unto him the Devil straight repayr's:
And boldly to revile him he begins,
Alledging that such prayr's are deadly sins;
And that it shewd, he was devoyd of grace,
To speake to God, from so unmeete a place.
The reverent man, though at the first dismaid;
Yet strong in faith, to Satan thus he said.
Thou damned spirit, wicked, false & lying,
Dispairing thine own good, & our envying:
Ech take his due, and me thou canst not hurt,
To God my pray'r I meant, to thee the durt,
Pure prayr ascends to him that high doth sit,
Down fals the filth, for fiends of hel more fit.

Harington installed one of his closets for his godmother in her palace at Richmond but there is no record of any other example of his excellent device—indeed, both he and his illustrious godmother were considered to be generally too clean for their own good in the land of the great unwashed; he bathing once a day and she 'once a month, whether she need it or no'.

William Hogarth *Night*

'Far overhead the windows opened, five, six, or ten storeys in the air, and the close stools of Edinburgh discharged the collected filth of the last twenty-four hours into the street. It was good manners for those above to cry "Gardy-loo!" (*Gardez l'eau*) before throwing. The returning roysterer cried back "Haud yer han", and ran with humped shoulders, lucky if his vast and expensive full-bottomed wig was not put out of action by a cataract of filth . . .'

G.M. Trevelyan
*English Social History*

'Tis want of sense to sup abroad too late
Unless thou first hast settled thy estate;
As many fates attend thy steps to meet
As there are waking windows in the street:
Bless the good gods and think thy chance is rare
To have a piss-pot only for thy share.

John Dryden.

Nearly two hundred years after Harington's bold attempts at sanitation, the water-closet struggled out of the mire once again. True, there had been isolated attempts by a few rich men to equip their simple privies with some kind of automatic sluicing system, but it wasn't until the 1770s that the first patent for a water-closet was taken out. There were three front-runners, and first round the bend was:

ALEXANDER CUMMINGS in 1775, closely followed by
SAMUEL PROSSER in 1777, and in hot pursuit
JOSEPH BRAMAH in 1778 (see illustration of his valve closet, right).

Once established, the wc went from strength to strength. By 1825, according to *Kelly's Price Book*, you could obtain a cheap valve closet all-inclusive for £3.10d. Competition grew fierce. Great names entered the field of plumbing: Humpherson, S.S. Hellyer, Crapper, Jennings, Bolding, Armitage Shanks and Thomas Twyford, seating the world's bottoms on china clay thrones with fanciful names like 'Beaufort', 'Optimus', 'Deluge', 'Unitas', 'Perfectus', 'Eureka', 'Desideratum' and 'Native Bombay'.

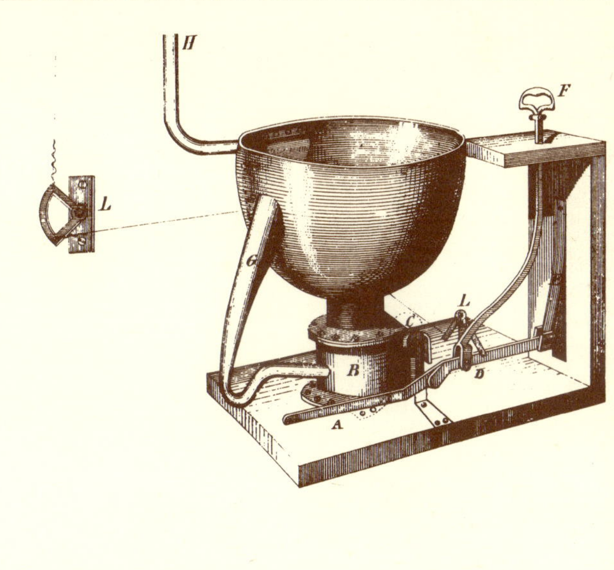

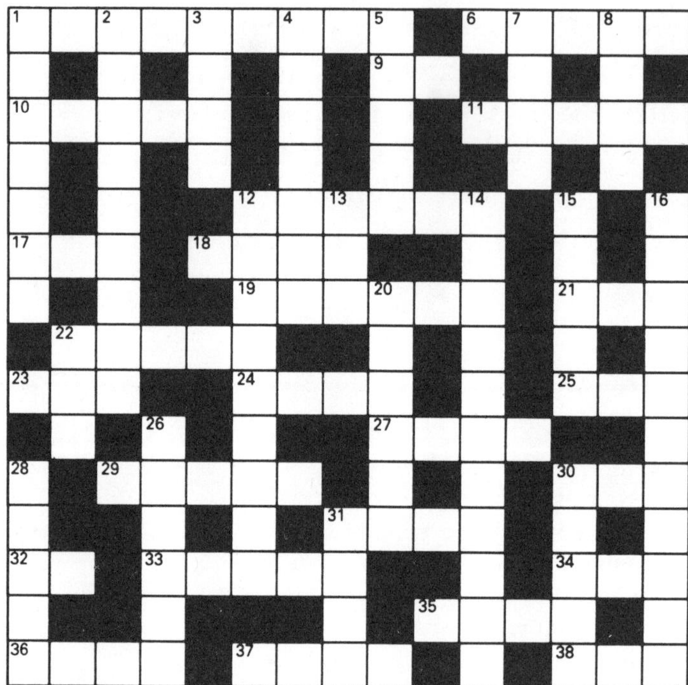

ACROSS

1 Are hair-do's tangled when breaking into a run? (9)
6 History of Art session includes a lot of hot air. (5)
9 The thing in question. (2)
10 Features detect 6 with these. (5)
11 Hot stuff! It could lead to 1 across or 6. (5)
12 'To ___ like a lady breeding' (Swift). (6)
17 Look round the privy. (3)
18 About a hundred repeated for little Pierre. (2-2)
19 Even with a duenna she could not go in here. (6)
21 Is able to carry it. (3)
22 Hand-held member is mightier than the sword. (5)
23 Gastronomy could begin, and end, with this. (3)
24 Beaufart scale? (4)
25 Men can stand women who do. (3)
27 Grecian 34's. (4)
29 Jobs lost because of strike in ship. (5)
30 Annoyingly, he gives me this, but I let this part of the tomato pass. (3)
31 English 19. (4)
32 Polluted river. (2)
33 The French have a word for it. (5)
34 Perhaps drop a brown one on the green baize. (3)
35 Colourful joke. (4)
36 Brings to pass. (4)
37 Result after one sips erratically. (4)
38 When stuck, this can drive one round the bend. (3)

DOWN

1 What the insect saw when the shit hit the fan. (4-3)
2 Earl's shoe is undone, although peers don't use these. (9)
3 Reckless nappy change could reveal this. (4)
4 Poor, if ice is found in the hole. (7)
5 Pointed 22 across before discharge. (5)
7 Janus loses his head getting to the bottom of it. (4)
8 We usually produce one a day, but particularly in the course of Saturday. (4)
12 Wear spats to confound the flow. (4,5)
13 Is the lavatory man desperate? (3)
14 'e is disturbed to see no fleas while one has to concentrate. (4,7)
15 With or without balls they are still a turn-on. (5)
16 If this, a difficult one to work out. (11)
20 Order U-bend to uncover excrement. (6)
22 A match put to 23 could cause a flash in here. (3)
26 Sceptical crapper. (6)
28 Cleaned out. (5)
30 Daily cleans up. (5)
31 Food, or the result of it. (4)

*For solution, see page opposite 'Ill Wind'.*

# OUT OF THE CLOSET

## (LOOSE TALK)

Oh Cloacina Goddess of this place,
Look on thy servant with a smiling face
Soft and cohesive let my offering flow
Not rudely swift nor obstinately slow.

Victorian poem.

*'Life is like a sewer. What you get out of it depends on what you put into it.'* Tom Lehrer

James Gilray *Sawney in the Bog-House*

*'Tis a bra' bonny Seat, 'o my Soul, Sawney cries,*
*I never beheld sic before with my Eyes,*
*Such a place in aw' Scotland I never could meet,*
*For the High and the Low ease themselves in the Street.'*

**ome observations on the state of rivers before the introduction of proper ewers and drainage:**

The river Rhine, it is well known,
oth wash your city of Cologne;
ut tell me, nymphs! What power divine
hall henceforth wash the river Rhine?'

S. T. Coleridge

Here strip my children! Here at once leap in!
Here prove who best can dash thro' thick and thin,
And who the most in love of dirt excel,
Or dark dexterity of groping well.

Alexander Pope, *Dunciad*

**Extracts from 'On a famous Voyage', (Epigramme 133, A fantasy journey along the abused and disgusting Fleet River), by Ben Jonson:**

A voice was heard, 'Cocytus.'
'Row close then, slaves.' 'Alas, they will beshite us.'
'No matter, stinkards, row. What croaking sound
Is this we hear? Of frogs?' 'No, guts wind-bound,
Over your heads': 'Well, row.' At this a loud
Crack did report itself, as if a cloud
Had burst with storm, and down fell, *ab excelsis*,
Poor Mercury, crying out on Paracelsus,
And all his followers, that had so abused him:
And, in so shitten sort, so long had used him:
For (where he was the god of eloquence,
And subtlety of metals) they dispense
His spirits, now, in pills, and eek in potions,
Suppositories, cataplasms, and lotions.

'How dare
Your dainty nostrils (in so hot a season,
When every clerk eats artichokes, and peason,
Laxative lettuce, and such windy meat)
'Tempt such a passage? When each privy's seat
Is filled with buttock? And the walls do sweat
Urine, and plasters? When the noise doth beat
Upon your ears, of discords so unsweet?
And outcries of the damnéd in the Fleet?

N.B. *Mercury was in use as a laxative in various forms until recently.*

**Charles Dickens vividly chronicles the polluted state of London's infamous Folly Ditch in *Oliver Twist*:**

At such times, a stranger looking from one of the wooden bridges thrown across it at Mill Lane, will see the inhabitants of the houses on either side lowering from their back doors and windows, buckets, pails, domestic utensils of all kinds, in which to haul the water up; and when his eye is turned from these operations to the houses themselves, his utmost astonishment will be excited by the scene before him. Crazy wooden galleries common to the backs of half a dozen houses, with holes from which to look out upon the slime beneath; windows, broken and patched, with poles thrust out, on which to dry the linen that is never there; rooms so small, so filthy, so confined, that the air would seem too tainted even for the dirt and squalor which they shelter; wooden chambers thrusting themselves out above the mud, and threatening to fall into it – as some have done; dirt-besmeared walls and decaying foundations; every repulsive lineament of poverty, every loathsome indication of filth, rot, and garbage; all these ornament the banks of Folly Ditch.

Whereas the natural functions of man were in previous ages a matter for open comment and discussion, as they are today among most nations other than our own, we suffer from this impediment in discussing these important matters, that among the English all relating to excretion is made a matter of euphemism.

Reginald Reynolds, *Cleanliness and Godliness*

# ANALOGUES

**privy**. 1375; mid. Eng. or old French *prive*.
**gong**. 14th century. cf Chaucer. *The Parson's Tale*.
**gong-house**. late 14th century.
**close-stool (house)**. 1410.
**siege**. *c.*1400.
**siege-house**. 1440.
**siege-hole**. 1447.
**the jakes** or **jacques**. 1530; poss. ex Jack's place.
**the jacks**. as above.
**Ajax**. 16th century; a pun on 'a jakes'.
**boggard**. 1552.
**bog**.
**bog-house**. 1670.
**bog-shop**. *c.*1840.
**the bogs**. *c.*1840 public-school slang.
**stool**. 1542
**draught**. 17th century.
**draught-chapel**. 17th century.
**house of office**. 17th century.
**necessary-vault**. 1609.
**necessary-house**. 1611.
**necessary-place**. 1697.
**croppin-ken**. 1676.
**little-house**. 1720.
**water-closet**. 1755.
**shot-tower**.
**closet of ease**. 1662.
**latrine**. 1642. French, ex Latin. *lavare*, to wash.
**necessary**. 1756.
**coffee-house**. late 18th century.
**coffee-shop**. late 18th century.
**le lieu**. French: the place.
**forakers**. 19th century. Winchester College.
**cloaca**. 1840. ex Cloacina, goddess of sewers.
**lavatory**. 1845. lit. a place for washing.
**lav**. Trinity College, Dublin.
**colfabas**. *c.*1820. Latinised Irish.
**crapping-casa, -ken**. 18th century; ex to crop; harvest.
**crapping-castle**. 19th century.
**crapping-house**. late 19th century.
**fourth**. mid 19th century, Cambridge slang; a note would be pinned on the undergraduate's door with the message: 'Gone[4]'.
**Quaker's burying ground**. 19th century.
**chamber of commerce**. 19th century.
**Jerry-come-tumble**. 1850.
**The West Central**. 1860.
**spice island**. *c.*1810.
**chapel (of ease)**. *c.*1860.
**closet**. 1869.
**Mrs Jones**. *c.*1860 euphemism.
**aunt Jones**. *c.*1870.
**aunt** (or **auntie**). *c.*1850.
**my aunt Jones**. *c.*1870.
**the place of general interest**. mid 19th century.
**casa**. mid 19th century. ex Latin, house.
**case**.
**crapping-case**. 1859.
**petty-house**. 19th century.
**where the Queen goes on foot**. late 19th century.
**where the Queen sends nobody**. late 19th century.
**the W**. late 19th century.
**W.C.** late 19th century. abbr. water closet.
**Sir John**. 19th century.
**dunnekin**. or **-ken**; late 19th century, ex dannaken.
**dunny**. 1860 Australian.
**thunderbox**. 1870 military esp. India.
**place of easement**. late 19th century.
**house of ease**. late 19th century.
**cacatorium**. late 19th century. ex latin *cacare*, to defecate.
**letter-box**. late 19th century.
**the Long.** late 19th century. Brasenose, Oxford: from benefactress, Lady Long.
**loo**. *c.*1900, ex French *l'eau*; ex gardy-loo (*gardez-vous de l'eau*).
**the temple of health**. late 19th century.
**dike** (also **dyke**). mid 19th century.
**cloakroom**.
**throneroom**.
**toilet**. ex French *toilette* (*toile*, cloth, dressing).
**cottage**. *c.*1900.
**didee**. *c.*1900 Australian.
**hoosegow**. 1911 (lit. a small prison).
**the place where you cough**. *c.*1920.
**(public) convenience**. 19th century.
**the back**. 19th century.
**dressing-room**. 20th century, Amer.
**boudoir**. 20th century Amer.
**Fred**. 20th century Amer.
**biffy**. 20th century Canadian.
**geography of the house**. 20th century.
**the John**. 20th century Amer.
**rear**. 1880 university slang.
**the heads**. late 19th century naval colloquialism.
**can**. 20th century Amer.
**crapper**. 20th century ex Thomas Crapper, sanitary engineer.
**crappus**. 20th century public school slang.
**tope**. ex Greek *topos*.
**the Styx**. Leys School, Cambridge.
**the woods**. Marlborough College.
**the groves**. Lancing.
**shants**.
**wasses**.
**japs**. Westminster School.
**cuzzes**. University slang, ex Hebrew.
**Obeum**. Cambridge. Ex initials of Oscar Browning.
**try-hards**. 20th century Cheltenham College.,
**urinal**. 20th century.
**piss-house**. 20th century.
**dags**. 20th century Australian.
**slash-house**. 20th century.
**slash-pit**. 20th century.
**slasher**. 20th century.
**snakes**. 20th century Australian.
**delhi**. 20th century girls' public school.
**karzi**. Hindustani.
**carzy**. prison slang.
**dubs**. 20th century.
**shit-house**.
**shitter**.
**shittus**.
**shooting gallery**.
**house of commons**. mid 19th century.
**little boys' (girls') room**. 1944 Amer.
**smallest room in the house**. 20th century Amer.
**urinary**. 1828.
**place of convenience**. 1883.
**fountain palace**. 1890 Amer.
**public comfort station**. 1904 Amer.
**where the (k)nobs hang out**. 19th century.
**powder-room**. 20th century Amer.
**rest-room**. 20th century Amer.
**wash-room**. 20th century Amer.
**forty-twa**. 1820 Scottish; from the number of seats.
**hoojy-boo**. attrib. to Dame Edith Evans.
**gents' toilet**.
**ladies' (room or toilet)**.
**men and women**.
**ladies and gentlemen**.
**gentlemen's smoking room**.
**ladies' retiring room**.
**gunroom**. 20th century Amer.
**his and hers**.
**Adam and Eve**.
**cocks and hens**.
**lads and lassies**.
**guys and dolls**.
**gulls and buoys**.

**I' front the Royal Exchange, and Underground,**
**Down gleaming walls of Porc'lain flows the sluice**
**That out of sight decants the kidney Juice,**
**Thus pleasuring those Gents for miles around,**
**Who, crying for relief, once piped the Sound**
**Of Wind in alleyways. All hail this news!**
**And let the joyous shuffling queues**
**For gentlemanly Jennings' most well-found**
**Construction, wherein a Penny opes the gate**
**To Heav'n's mercy; and sanitary Wares**
**Receive the Gush with seemly, cool obedience,**
**Enthroning Queen Hygeia in blessed State**
**On Crapper's Rocket; With rapturous ease Men's cares**
**Shall flow away when seated at Convenience!**

Josiah Feable, *'to commemorate the opening of the first Underground Public Convenience at the Royal Exchange by George Jennings in 1855'.*

It was a raw day in January and the big public lavatory was very cold.

'It's freezing down here,' shivered a passer-through to the old attendant.

'Yers,' agreed the old man, 'it's bein' 'as 'ow it's underground, an' then there's all the cold water and the stone floors, and the tiles on the wall.'

'Why don't you get yourself a paraffin stove?' said the customer.

'What!' exclaimed the old man, 'and stink the place out!'

## From *Unreliable Memoirs* by Clive James

Ever since I could remember, the dunny man had come running down the driveway once a week. From inside the house, we could hear his running footsteps. Then we could hear the rattle and thump as he lifted the lavatory, took out the full pan, clipped on a special lid, and set down an empty pan in its place. After more rattling and banging, there was an audible intake of breath as he hefted the full pan on to his shoulder. Then the footsteps went back along the driveway, slower this time but still running. From outside in the street there was rattling, banging and shouting as the full pan was loaded on to the dunny cart along with all the other full pans. I often watched the dunny cart from the front window. As it slowly made its noisome way down the street, the dunny men ran to and from it with awesome expertise. They wore shorts, sandshoes, and nothing else except a sun-tan suspiciously deep on the forearms. Such occasional glimpses were all one was allowed by one's parents and all that was encouraged even by the dunny men themselves. They preferred to work in nobody's company except their own. They were a band apart. . . .

From day to day it got fuller and fuller, generating maggots by about the third day. To combat the smell, honeysuckle was grown on a trellis outside the lavatory door, in the same way that the European nobility had recourse to perfume when they travelled by galley. The maggots came from blowflies and more blowflies came from the maggots. Blowflies were called blowies. The Australian climate, especially on the Eastern seaboard in the latitude of Sydney, was specifically designed to accommodate them. The blowies' idea of a good time was to hang around the dunny waiting for the seat to be lifted. They were then faced with the challenge of getting through the hole before it was blocked by the descending behind of the prospective occupant. There was no time for any fancy flying. Whether parked on the wall or stacking around in a holding pattern near the ceiling, every blowie was geared up to make either a vertical dive from high altitude or a death-defying low-level run through the rapidly decreasing air-space between the seat and your descending

arse. The moment the seat came up, suddenly it was Pearl Harbour.

My mother and I were having breakfast. I heard the dunny man's footsteps thumping along the driveway, with a silent pause as he hurdled my bicycle, which in my habitual carelessness I had left lying there. I heard the usual thumps, bangs and heaves. I could picture the brimming pan, secured with the special clipped lid, hoisted high on his shoulder while he held my mother's gift bottle of beer in his other, appreciative hand. Then the footsteps started running back the other way. Whether he forgot about my bicycle, or simply mistimed his jump, there was no way of telling. Suddenly there was the noise of . . . well, it was mainly the noise of a dunny man running full tilt into a bicycle. The uproar was made especially ominous by the additional noise – tiny but significant in context – of a clipped lid springing off.

While my mother sat there with her hands over her eyes I raced out through the fly-screen door and took a look down the driveway. The dunny man, overwhelmed by the magnitude of his tragedy, had not yet risen to his feet. Needless to say, the contents of the pan had been fully divulged. All the stuff had come out. But what was really remarkable was the way none of it had missed him. Already you could hear a gravid hum in the air. Millions of flies were on their way towards us. They were coming from all over Australia. For them, it was a Durbar, a moot, a gathering of the clans. For us, it was the end of an era.

Two workmen were knee-deep in a sewer, one carrying his sandwiches buttoned inside his shirt. When he bent to unclear a blockage his lunch slipped out and fell into the thick. With a snort of exasperation he was forced to delve up to his elbows to retrieve his lost lunch. It took a couple of minutes to bring it to the light and, wiping it more or less clean on his trousers, he took a bite.

'Ugh!' he retched, his eyes watering. 'Bloody cheese again!'

Why Strephon will you tell the rest?
And must you needs describe the Chest?
That careless Wench! no Creature warn her
To move it out from yonder Corner;
But leave it standing full in Sight
For you to exercise your Spight.
In vain, the Workman shew'd his Wit
With Rings and Hinges counterfeit
To make it seem in this Disguise,
A Cabinet to vulgar Eyes;
Which Strephon ventured to look in,
Resolv'd to go through thick and thin,
He lifts the Lid there need no more,
He smelt it all the Time before.

Jonathan Swift, 'The Lady's Dressing Room'.

The club was old and distinguished, and so was the membership. The rooms were spacious and tall, the furniture large and heavy: massive lamps, deep-buttoned leather, glowing mahogany.

For some strange reason the only serious attempt at modernisation had been a complete refitting of the lavatory. Gone the gigantic 'horse-stall' urinals, and in their place more compact porcelain sentinels – neat, sharp-lined, with angled smoked glass at the base, to protect the shoes from rogue spray.
Gone the vast cisterns and their china-handled chains, and instead slim, low-level tanks, with push-button flush . . . silent, almost noiseless. On the walls pink tiles and tinted mirrors, below them built-in wash basins with sparkling chrome taps.

Two of the elder members – the old, even among the old – stood at the urinal in the trickling silence of slow relief.

'Lovely in here, isn't it?' said the first. 'Very lovely, now it's all been done up so fine.'

'Yes,' replied the other. 'Very nice indeed . . . Trouble is, it makes yer cock look a bit shabby.'

Dan, Dan, the lavatory man
Working underground all day.
In the urinals, picking up the finals,
Happy as the flowers in May.
Poor old chap,
Picking up the crap,
He can't tell shit from clay!

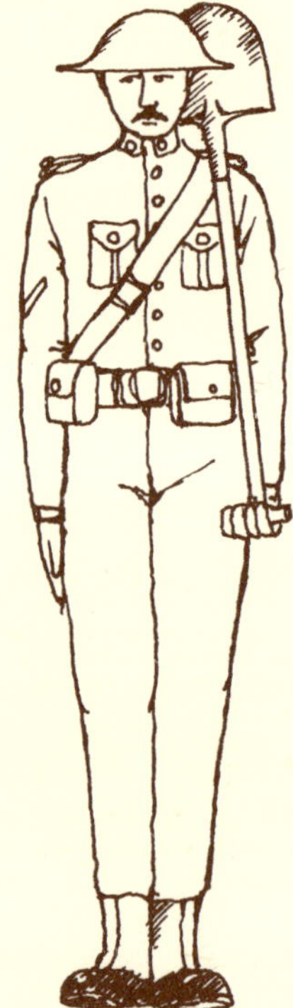

*Field Service Pocket Book*, 1914.

**8. Latrines, urinals, refuse pits, horse and cattle lines, and slaughtering places must be placed as far as possible from the kitchens, from any source of water supply, and to leeward if possible. They must never be placed in any gullies which, when it rains, may discharge into the water supply. A sanitary policeman should be placed in charge of each latrine, his duty being to see that every man covers up his excreta with earth. Failure to carry out this practice should be punished.**

They took it there, fifty yards away. It was less commodious than the hut, but Apthorpe said it would do. As they were returning from their adventure he paused in the path and said with unusual warmth: 'I shan't forget this evening's work, Crouchback. Thank you very much.' . . .

After a few more steps Apthorpe said: 'Look here, old man, if you'd care to use the thunder-box, too, it's all right with me.'

It was a moment of heightened emotion; an historic moment, had Guy recognized it, when in their complicated relationship Apthorpe came nearest to love and trust. It passed, as such moments do between Englishmen.

'It's very good of you but I'm quite content as I am.'

'Sure?'

'Yes.'

'That's all right then,' said Apthorpe, greatly relieved.

Thus Guy stood high in Apthorpe's favour and became with him joint custodian of the thunder-box.

Evelyn Waugh, *Men at Arms.*

**At a certain Army barracks during the Second World War, a type of latrine existed which resembled a flute. It consisted of a drainage pipe with large holes at regular intervals, each of which was a kind of water-closet. The stock joke was to drop a lighted newspaper in the hole at the far end of the pipe and allow it to float along, causing considerable surprise and alarm to those seated on the other holes.**

**Ex-acting captain, Royal Warwickshire Regiment**

I well remember how embarrassed we were as recruits in barracks when we had to use the general latrine. There were no doors and twenty men sat side by side as in a railway carriage, so that they could be reviewed all at one glance, for soldiers must always be under supervision . . .

Here in the open air, though, the business is entirely a pleasure. I no longer understand why we should always have shied at it before. It is, in fact, just as natural as eating and drinking . . .

The soldier is on friendlier terms than other men with his stomach and intestines. Three-quarters of his vocabulary is derived from these regions, and they give an intimate flavour to expressions of his greatest joy as well as of his deepest indignation . . .

Enforced publicity has in our eyes restored the character of innocence to all these things. More than that, they are so much a matter of course that their comfortable performance is fully as much enjoyed as the playing of a safe top-running flush. Not for nothing was the word 'latrine-humour' invented; these places are the regimental gossip-shops and common-rooms.

Erich Maria Remarque, *All Quiet on the Western Front.*

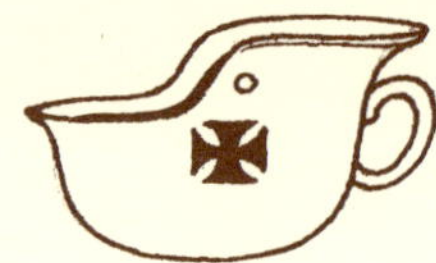

Two plumbers were doing some maintenance work in a sewer. Suddenly one of them slipped from the ledge on which they were working and plunged some twenty feet into the effluent which swirled below.
'Gawd Fred!' Are you all right?' shouted the man above.
'Yers,' came back the faint cry.
' 'ang on, I'll get a rope,' said his mate. 'Can you swim?'
'Nah,' said Fred, 'but I'm going through the motions.'

**From *Ending Up* by Kingsley Amis**

Some hours later, Bernard stood by the just-open door of his bedroom. He was unusually accoutred, with a damp washing-flannel slung across his face in the yashmak position – it was secured at the back of his head by a safety-pinned stretch of elastic purloined from Adela's work-box – a pair of bellows in one hand and a dustpan and brush in the other. On his bedside table, the radio was loudly relaying some carol or other. Marigold made her fleeting appearance. The nearby door duly shut and the key turned. Bernard moved into action.

He laid down his implements by the small door in question and took from his pocket a small transparent sphere. This he placed as near as possible to the crack under the door, a chink measuring nearly a quarter of an inch, and crushed it noiselessly under the dustpan. At once a terrible and tremendous odour was released, so strong as to penetrate easily his improvised gas-mask. Retching almost continuously, he worked hard with the bellows to blow into the lavatory every possible molecule of vapour. He kept this up for twenty seconds or so, then rapidly and efficiently swept up the fragments.

A call came from George's bedroom down the landing. 'I say! Bernard, are you there? Bernard?'

'Coming.'

He was with George after a very short delay, his various tools safely hidden for the moment under Shorty's bed.

'I say, Bernard, what on earth is this frightful stink? Oh, merry Christmas, old boy.'

'Merry Christmas, George. I've no idea.'

'Could you open that window as wide as it'll go? It really is awful. What can it be?'

Bernard did as he was asked. 'Well . . . the only thing I can think of . . . I did happen to notice Marigold going into the bog.'

The left half of George's face expressed incredulity. 'But you don't mean . . . Surely no human . . . It's not like any ordinary . . .'

'Not ordinary, no. But she has been under the doctor. I suppose there may be something . . .'

'It smells to me like a stink-bomb.'

'Really? I don't think I've ever—'

'We used to muck about with them at school. Phew! Actually it is beginning to die down a bit.'

It had died down a good deal further by the time Marigold came into the room. She wished them a merry Christmas and kissed them both. It came natural to her to kiss George; Bernard she kissed partly because she hoped to shame him by doing so without the least hint of overt reluctance, partly because she knew he disliked being touched by anyone, and partly because the impending arrival of the young people made her feel generally benevolent.

'Funny smell in here,' she said, sniffing. 'I noticed it out there too.'

'Yes, we were wondering what it was,' said Bernard.

'I expect it's the drains. I'll tell Adela. Well, I must be on my way. See you downstairs soon, I hope, George.'

'Rum go, that,' said George when she had left. 'You'd have thought she'd have noticed it most when she was, well, closest to the drains. I think you can shut the window now, if you would.'

Bernard again obeyed. He did not try to speak. So much for his hopes of suggesting to Marigold that her insides had started to decompose! The patent and total failure of Operation Stink was mainly due to two factors unknown to him. He had not risked an indoor trial, and his outdoor one, while useful in establishing the fragility of the capsules, had told him nothing of the speed with which their contents were dispersed; thus only a small fraction of the gas had ever got into the lavatory. And that small fraction had been promptly blown out again by the draught from its window, which the fastidious Marigold invariably threw open on arrival there.

Bernard's Christmas was off to a bad start.

According to the ancient laws of Manu, every conceivable part of the body was liable to be amputated as a punishment, including the anus of any citizen who might break wind in front of the king.
Guido Majno, *The Healing Hand: Man and Wound in the Ancient World*

Now that she was alone she would have to have the catch put back on the shutters. Tusker had had it taken off for the same reason that he had insisted on two loos. In India, he had said, you could never tell when you'd get taken short. And who could tell if you both might not get taken short at the same moment? If they could only have one bathroom, they could at least have two loos in it and no catch on the door. Actually it had only happened once, the time they'd both eaten something that disagreed with them. She'd always sworn she'd never undergo the indignity of sitting on her loo while Tusker was sitting on his. But, this once, she'd been driven to it, and half way through the performance Tusker had begun to laugh and after a while she had begun to laugh too, so there they had been, enthroned, laughing like drains.

Paul Scott, *Staying On*

# JOB LOT

## (GOING, GOING...)

**Sir Hugh Evans.** 'If there is one, I shall make two in the company.'

**Doctor Gaius.** 'If there be one or two, I shall make-a the turd.'

*The Merry Wives of Windsor* (Act 3, scene 3),
William Shakespeare.

## IN ROUNDELAY

In shitting yesterday I did know
The sess I to my arse did owe:
The smell was such came from that slunk,
That I was with it all bestunk:
O had but then some brave Signor
Brought her to me I waited for.
In shitting!
I would have cleft her water-gap,
And join'd it close to my flip-flap;
Whilst she had with her fingers guarded
My foul nockandrow, all bemerded
In shitting.

Rabelais, *Gargantua.*

A Frenchman came home late at night covered in *merde*. It was all over his head and running down his face. '*Sacré bleu*!' said his wife. 'How did you get like that, *chéri*?' 'Oooolala,' he replied. 'My beret blew off my head in the dark and landed in Père Auguste's cow-field. I tried nine on before I found my own!'

### PECUNIA OLET

**In April 1974 the Arts Council staged an exhibition at the Serpentine Gallery in London entitled 'From Barrie Bates to Billy Apple'. The theme of the exhibition was the tenuous relationship between Life and Art.**

**Paul Stileman, writing in the catalogue, states: 'Billy Apple has gone further; he has brought life and art so close together that only a tissue of thought stands between them.' Indeed, tissues played a large part in the show [an accumulation of nose and toilet tissues collected from the first nose blowing and bowel movement activity of each day, each one documented and recorded], as did ear-wax extractions, nose bleeds and semen-soaked tissues resulting from masturbation, of which there were 65 exhibits. However, when the show opened to the public on 6 April, all the 'bowel tissues' had been removed, presumably on the grounds of 'taste'.**

# ANALOGUES

# (NUMBER TWO)

**turd** (11th century ex Anglo-Saxon, *tord*; a germanic radical; ex Latin *tordere*.
**go to siege** *c.*1400.
**shite** 14th century ex French *chier*; ex German *scheissen*, to shit.
**shit** 15th century.
**(do one's) stools** 1542.
**evacuate (the bowels)** 1607.
**perform the work of nature** 1607.
**faeces** 1639.
**excrete** 1668.
**ease nature** 1701.
**thorough-go-nimble** 1694.
**ease oneself** 18th century.
**poop** 18th century.
**obey the call(s) of nature** 1747.
**crap** Mid 18th century ex crop; to take in the harvest.
**pass one's stools** 1799.
**do one's pieces**.
**ordure**.
**bury a Quaker** *c.*1800 Anglo-Irish.
**on the pot** 1810 nursery.
**go to bog** 1811.
**do one's business** 1850.
**do a dike** Mid 19th century.
**defecate** 1864.
**to bog** 1870.
**chuck a turd** 19th century.
**poo-poo** 19th century nursery.
**do (or go) potty** 19th century
**rear** 1890 university slang; also military: a man 'taken short' was told to 'fall out to the rear'.
**clear one's bowels**.
**do one's tables** 19th century.
**go to Sir Harry** 19th century.
**visit Sir John** 19th century.
**cack** Late 19th century. Ex Latin *cacare*.
**ca-ca**.
**go round the back** Late 19th century; from the days of backyard privies.
**go round the haystack** Late 19th century rhyming slang.
**horse and trap** Late 19th century rhyming slang.
**do a bunk**.
**do a shift** 1865.
**do a rural** 1860.
**do-do** Late 19th century.
**drown a mole** 20th century.
**pony and trap**.
**do a dunneken** Late 19th century.
**concentrate** Late 19th century.
**quiet time** Late 19th century.
**do a job** (for oneself) Late 19th century.
**make chamber music** Late 19th century.
**pass a motion** *c.*1900.
**go and post a letter** (20th century)
**go and sing 'Sweet Violets'**
**do something no-one else can do**
**relieve oneself**.
**shoot oneself** 19th century, applied to someone who has farted (shot himself) with the rejoinder 'If he's not careful he'll shit himself.'
**big hit** 1920 Australian rhyming slang.
**tom tit** Early 20th century rhyming slang.
**my word!** 20th century rhyming slang; 'my word, I trod in a "my word".'
**strangle a darkie** 20th century Australian.
**plops** 20th century nursery, echoic.
**ah-ah** 20th century nursery, echoic.
**number two** 20th century nursery.
**big jobs** 20th century nursery.
**jobs**.
**jobbies**.
**bigs**
**dump**.
**banger**.
**lurker**.
**bobber**.
**floater**.

**collywobbles**.
**to have the (drizzling) shits**.
**squits**.
**squitters** Mid 17th century.
**the runs** 19th century.
**back-door trots** 19th century.
**the trots**.
**Jimmy Britts** 20th century Australian; rhyming slang.
**the jimmys**.
**jerry-go nimble**.
**Franco's revenge**.
**Summer complaint**.

**let off** 20th century.
**blow off** 20th century.
**free a nigger** Early 20th century American.
**pass wind** 19th century.
**pump** 19th century Scottish.
**wind the horn**.
**bullock's heart** (rhyming slang).
**horse and cart** 20th century rhyming slang.
**tom tart** 20th century rhyming slang.
**heart and dart** Mid 19th century.
**shoot a bunny** 20th century.

When one urinates or defecates, one must squat in a way that neither faces, nor turns away from, Mecca.

It is forbidden to defecate in the following places: on the property of someone who has not given his permission, in any holy place, or in the tombs of the faithful. It is best to avoid squatting facing the sun or moon, even if the genitals are covered; in a place exposed to the wind; on the doorstep of a house; under a fruit-tree.

It is preferable to urinate or defecate squatting in a private place and to enter this place with the left foot and leave it with the right; it is recommended that one covers one's head during evacuation and supports the weight of one's body on the left foot.

When one urinates or defecates, one must hide one's genitalia from the eyes of anyone who has reached the age of puberty, including one's mother, one's sister, the feeble-minded and any child who is old enough to understand. One does not have to hide one's genitalia from one's husband or wife.

It is not necessary to hide one's genitalia with anything in particular; one's hand will suffice.

Ayatollah Khomeiny, *Political, Philosophical, Social and Religious Principles.*

Recommended position, showing strong Russian influence

Shittard
Squittard
Crakard
  Turdous,
Thy bung
Hath flung
Some dung
  On us:
Filthard
Cackard
Stinkard,
  St Anthony's fire
  seize on thy toane,
If thy
Dirty
Dounby
  Thou do not wipe,
  ere thou be gone.

Rabelais, *Gargantua*.

**The first aeroplane fitted with a lavatory was the giant Russian passenger transport *Russky Vitiaz*, designed by Igor Sikorski and test flown at Petrograd on 13 May 1913. Whether this was a water-closet proper is doubtful, as it seems unlikely that Sikorski would have increased the load by carrying unnecessary supplies of water. It is nevertheless recorded here as a tribute to the first man who concerned himself with the problems of high-altitude sanitation.**

*The Shell Book of Firsts*

**In the 1930s *Pravda* inadvertently printed 'Sralin' instead of Stalin. As 'sral' is the past tense of 'srat', to shit, and 'sralin' literally means 'shitting man', everyone remotely connected with this typographical error, from copy-desk to printshop, was arrested. They were then sent to a charming little place on the Gulag archipelago.**

A man is taken short in an hotel room, and the toilet at the end of the corridor is occupied. He rushes back to his bedroom, defecates in a paper bag and goes to throw it out of the window. As he lifts the bag to throw it, the bottom rips and the shit splatters all up the wall behind him and across the ceiling. Horrified by the mess he has created, he calls up the hotel-porter and offers him five dollars to clean things up and tell no one. The porter looks the room over carefully and says, 'You know what, boss? I'll give you *ten* dollars if you tell me how you did it.'

Little birdie flying high
Dropped a message from the sky
An angry farmer wiped his eye
Said, 'What a blessin' cows don't fly.'

From time to time we are called upon to describe our motions to an interested party – a doctor, perhaps, or a nanny, a mother or an aunt. Here is a handy chart for quick reference:

Jaws

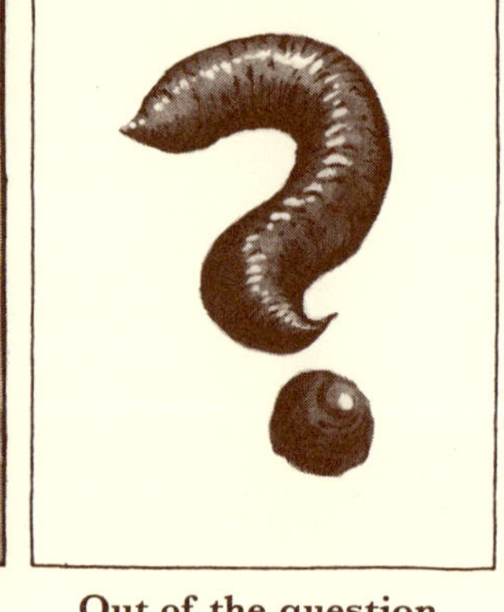

Out of the question

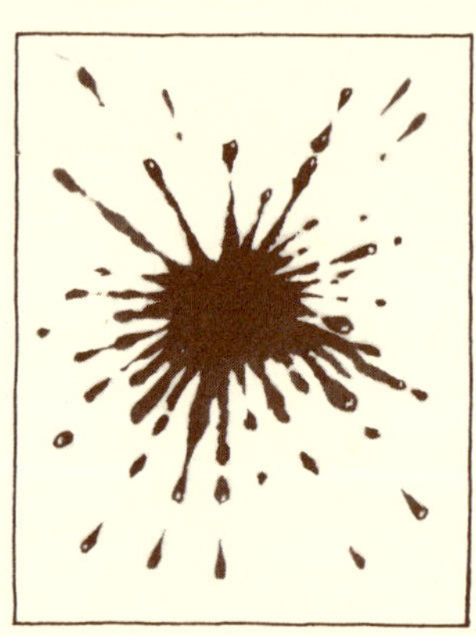

Tooloose Lautrec

Cottage loaf

Doppel-bänger

Bobber

Floater

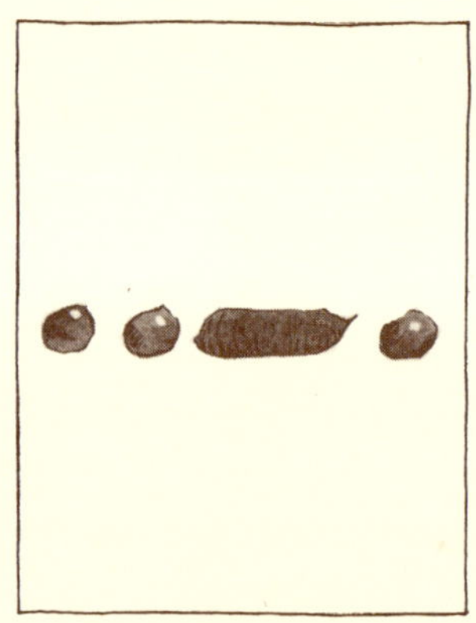

Morse

## NEAPOLITAN LYRIC

| | |
|---|---|
| Strunz' . . . | Turd . . . |
| Nel sole fumante | You smoke in the sun |
| Come un incenso | Like an incense burner |
| A Dio . . . | To God . . . |
| Una mosca | A fly |
| Ti canta | Sings you |
| Una ninna-nanna . . . | A lullaby . . . |
| Zzz . . . Zzz . . . | Zzz . . . Zzz . . . |
| Ma . . . tu non ascolti . . . | But . . . you don't listen . . . |
| Strunz' . . . | Turd |

Ev'n them he canna get attended,
Altho' their face he ne'er had kend it,
Just shit in a kail-blade* an' send it,
As soon's he smells 't,
Baith their disease and what will mend it,
At once he tells 't.

Robert Burns, 'Death and Dr Hornbrook'.

* cabbage-leaf

We were on this luxury yacht I'd chartered from a Lord and in the party was a financial whizz-kid renowned for doing these huge turds. One morning we were all desperate to answer the after-breakfast-call and he was stuck in the bog for hours. 'I can't get it to go,' he yelled, 'it keeps lurking back . . . God, it's like *Jaws* . . .' and then, after an age, the door burst open and he squealed 'Thank God I've done it! Broke its back with a tooth-brush.'

We never did find out whose toothbrush or which end.

'Doctor, my brother is a really heavy smoker. He smokes cigars all day and I'm worried about his health. How can I cure him of the habit?'

'Well, I'll tell you what to do. Get a box of his cigars, stick the ends up your arse, twist them round and put them back in the box. He'll soon go off the taste, believe me.'

The man does as he's told, and three weeks later he's back.

'Did it work?' asks the doctor.
'Oh yes,' says the man. 'He's given up smoking completely.'
'Well, why are you back here?' asks the physician.
'To see if you can cure me of this desperate urge to stick cigars up my bum.'

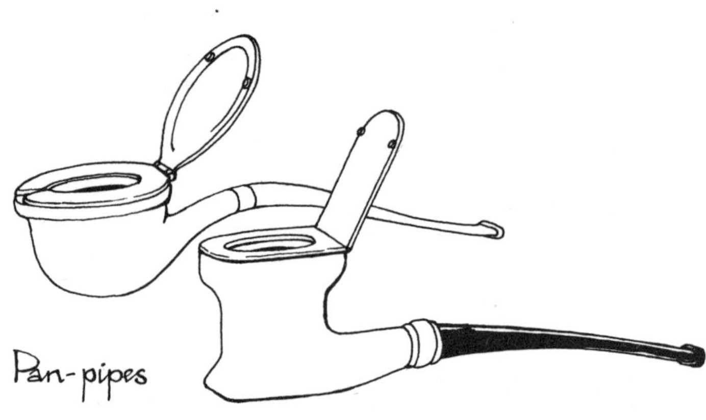


Q. Why are turds tapered?

A. To stop your arse shutting with a bang.

*'The Eagle shits today'.*
*(American service parlance denoting payday)*
*Also 'the crow shits'.*

## Some thoughts of Sigmund Freud:

We have been able to study transformations of instinct and similar processes particularly in anal erotism, the excitations arising from the sources of the erotogenic anal zone . . . It may not be easy, perhaps, to get free from the contempt into which this particular zone has fallen in the course of evolution. Let us therefore allow ourselves to be reminded by Abraham that embryologically the anus corresponds to the primitive mouth, which has migrated down to the end of the bowel. We have learnt, then, that after a person's own faeces, his excrement, has lost its value for him, this instinctual interest derived from the anal source passes over on to objects that can be presented as gifts. And this is rightly so, for faeces were the first gift that an infant could make, something he could part with out of love for whoever was looking after him. After this, corresponding exactly to analogous changes of meaning that occur in linguistic development, this ancient interest in faeces is transformed into the high valuation of *gold* and *money* but also makes a contribution to the affective cathexis of *baby* and *penis*. It is a universal conviction among children, who long retain the cloaca theory, that babies are born from the bowel like a piece of faeces: defaecation is the model of the act of birth.

*Definitions*

*copro*: prefix meaning 'excrement' or 'dung'.
*coprolalia*: obsessive obscene speech.
*coprophilia*: tendency to be interested in faeces.

## A COCKNEY BALLAD

A dirty old woman in London did dwell
That dirty old woman I knew her so well
She went to a Doctor for she couldn't shite
And he gave her a pill which was like dynamite
It was brown brown dirty old brown.

That dirty old woman she came home to bed
She jumped on her knees and she stood on her head
She stretched for the po but the po couldn't grasp
So she upped with the window and popped out her arse
It was brown brown dirty old brown.

A London policeman was walking his beat
Was walking his beat at the end of the street
He looked up above at the stars in the sky
When a bloody great turd hit him slap in the eye
It was brown brown dirty old brown.

That London policeman he cursed and he swore
He called that old woman all sorts of a whore
On the London Bridge now you can see him by night
With a card round his neck 'I was blinded by shite'
It was brown brown dirty old brown.

# HIT AND MISS
# (PEES AND QUEUES)

ON A LADY WHO P——ST
AT THE TRAGEDY OF CATO
Alexander Pope

While Maudlin Whigs deplor'd their *Cato's* Fate,
Still with dry Eyes the Tory *Celia* sate,
But while her Pride forbids her Tears to flow,
The gushing Waters find a Vent below:
Tho' secret, yet with copious Grief she mourns,
Like twenty River-Gods with all their Urns.
Let others screw their Hypocritick Face,
She shows her Grief in a sincerer Place;
There Nature reigns, and Passion void of Art,
For that Road leads directly to the Heart.

**MARIE LLOYD** used to sing a song containing the line: 'She sits among the cabbages and peas.' Stuffed-shirts, finding the double meaning of the last word offensive, brought pressure to bear, and finally Marie was obliged to change it. Instead she sang: 'She sits among the cabbages and leeks.'

The Winter Sky began to frown;
Poor Stella must pack off to Town.
From purling Streams and Fountains bubbling,
To Liffey's stinking Tide in Dublin:
From wholesome Exercise and Air
To sossing in an easy Chair;
From Stomach sharp and hearty Feeding
To piddle like a Lady breeding.

Jonathan Swift (1667–1745), 'Cadenus and Vanessa'.

Aerodynamic experts at Pan-American Airlines are currently working on a vital new area of study – the design of a new lavatory seat.

The problem arose on a recent Pan-American flight when a stout lady became involved in a conflict of pressures and air currents while she was sitting on the lavatory. The fact that at 30,000 ft. she completely covered the seat caused extraordinary aerodynamic suctions to build up with the result that she became wedged.

The combined efforts of two stewards failed to dislodge her and eventually the captain was called from the cockpit. Even he, stout fellow that he was, was unable to move the mountain of flesh.

Finally he was compelled to take his plane right down to below 5,000 ft. where, with reduced 'pressure differential' the good lady was shot off.

*PRIVATE EYE* No. 134, 3 Feb. 1967.

EVENING PRAYER
Arthur Rimbaud

An angel in the barber's hands, that's me. I squat
my life away, clutching a profoundly fluted pint,
cheroot betwixt my teeth, belly and shoulders bent,
the sky a pall of clouds intangibly distraught.

But dreams, like sun-warm droppings in a disused dove-cote,
swarm through my mind, with sweet, peppery content,
till moments come when my soft heart's like a laburnum lambent
in spring with the golden spill the April showers have wrought.
But when I've tucked away all those dreams and cleaned the plate
I shuffle out with thirty or forty pints in my skin, I confess
I'm obliged to seek ease for my bladder before it's too late.
And there you have me, meek as Jesus of hyssop and cedar cross
as I pee up into those dun skies, so lofty, so far, so remote, and
see, in approval, how the heliotrope blossoms toss.

***BAIGA*: A drink from the Gobi Desert which is made up of Millet and Pigeon Droppings which are mixed together and heated in small metal pots. The resultant liquor is extraordinarily potent.**
** **Our research showed it to be less alcoholic made with Budgie Droppings.***

My friend and I had digs where the landlady used to sneak in and drink our sherry. We took to marking the bottle, and finally my friend got madder and madder and started filling it up in his own particular way. It still kept going down – you can imagine, we laughed like drains.

When we were leaving she confessed to having 'borrowed' a nip now and then to put in our favourite sherry trifle.

An actor.

# ANALOGUES

## (NUMBER ONE)

**piss** Ex french, *pisser*; probably echoic.
**urinate** (1599).
**piddle** Late 18th century.
**diddle**.
**dicky diddle**.
**Jimmy Riddle** 19th century rhyming slang.
**Jerry**.
**pee** Late 18th century a softened version of piss.
**pee-pee** Late 19th century nursery.
**pee-wee** 19th century nursery.
**wee-wee** Late 19th century.
**cis-cis**.
**gig**.
**tinkle** 20th century echoic.
**sprinkle**.
**widdle**.
**wag**.
**micturate**
**long tea** 1850 schoolboy.
**make water** (1375).
**rattle and hiss** 1944 American.
**hit and miss** 20th century American.
**snake's hiss** Early 20th century.
**you and me** 19th century Australian.
**on the ooze** 1918.
**drain one's tatters**.
**strain one's taters**.
**inspect the plumbing**.
**disappear for a moment**.
**see a man about a dog**.
**see one's aunt**.
**make a call**.
**pay a call**.
**pass water**
**spend a penny**
**be excused**.
**pump** 18th century.
**pump ship** 1708 nautical.
**pump one's bilges**.
**shed a tear for Nelson**.
**(have a) slash** 20th century
**point Percy at the porcelain** 20th century Australian.
**point Alice at the Armitage** 20th century Australian.
**shake hands with the wife's best friend** 20th century Australian.
**pull out the one-eyed trouser snake** 20th century Australian.
**splash one's boots**.
**visit the snakes** 20th century Australian.
**Mrs Chant** 20th century cf 'Aunt'.
**number one**.
**little job**.
**wash one's hands**.
**powder one's nose**.
**squeeze the lemon**.
**have a run off** (*c.*1930).
**draw off** (20th century).
**rack off** (late 19th century from wine-making).
**wring one's socks out**.
**do a puddle**.
**whizzie**.
**pluck a rose** (18th century).
**pick a daisy** (*c.*1860).
**leak** (*c.*1590).
**have a leak** (Mid 19th century).
**do (or plant) a sweet-pea** (mid 19th century).
**water the nag** (mid 19th century).
**water one's dragon** (mid 19th century).
**shake hands with an old friend** (*c.*1880).
**shoot a lion** (*c.*1880).
**spend a penny** (*c.*1880).
**shake hands with the bloke one enlisted with** (mil. 2nd World War).
**do a sip** back-slang for piss.
**sip** 1903.
**apple and pip** rhyming slang on sip.
**turn the bike round** 20th century.
**see if the horse has lost its blanket** 20th C.

**Marghanita Laski evokes the appalling prudishness of an era when even piano legs were covered in this claustrophobic description from *The Victorian Chaise-Longue*, in which a modern girl is transported back in time during a nightmare:**

Melanie lifted her left hand, slowly and with difficulty, and twitched the brass bell from off the tatting . . . When Adelaide came into the room, the bell was lying on the coverlet, loosely held by Melanie's weak fingers.

'Well?' asked Adelaide, and bent over and replaced the bell upright on the tatting beside the tumbler.

'I want—' began Melanie, 'I want – I'm afraid that I must—' She was choking with shame, and could not go on. . . .

To the right, Melanie could see the corner of what appeared to be a white marble washstand-top, and here Adelaide disappeared from view; returning soon through the double-doors, carrying, under a white cloth, a chamber-pot.

The next minutes were darkened by blinding embarrassment. These actions, although so many times performed, were intolerable to both women, and when they were over, and Adelaide had carried away the chamber-pot, covered again by its decorous cloth, Melanie was lying back distraught and with her eyes shut, trying to blot out not the constant nightmare but the memory of shame beyond anything she had ever felt or conceived.

## *ADRIAN MITCHELL'S FAMOUS WEAK BLADDER BLUES*

Now some praise God because he gave us the bomb to drop in 1945
But I thank the Lord for equipping me with the fastest cock alive.

You may think a sten-gun's frequent, you can call greased lightning fast,
But race them down to the Piccadilly bog and watch me zooming past.

Well it's excuse me,
And I'll be back.
Door locked so rat-a-tat-tat.
You mind if I go first?
I'm holding this cloudburst.
I'll be out in 3.7 seconds flat.

I've got the Adamant Trophy, the Niagara Cup, you should see me on the
M.1. run,
For at every comfort station I've got a reputation for—doing the ton.

Once I met that Speedy Gonzales and he was first through the door.
But I was unzipped, let rip, zipped again and out before he could even draw.

Now God killed Vicky and he let Harold Wilson survive,
But the good Lord blessed little Adrian Mitchell with the fastest cock alive.

Before his execution Sir Thomas More . . . being told that he must prepare to die, for he could not live, called for his urinal, and having made water in it *he cast it and viewed it (as physicians do)* a pretty while; at last he swore soberly that he saw nothing in that man's water, but that he might live, if it pleased the King.

Reginald Reynolds, *Cleanliness and Godliness*

First, have *you* a personal plumbing problem? If not, you are lucky, because medical statistics show that six men out of ten have some form of urinary ailment after the age of sixty.

Boisterous, healthy young man. You who function so perfectly in all departments, take heed! (Actually, there is nothing else you can take.) Scorn not the pitiful creature who must have a seat near the exit. One day this prudence may be your necessity. Laugh not, and remember that pennies are sometimes spent at half-hourly intervals by day and night.

This may happen to you – if you belong to the six.

Against the possible attack of Frequency no man is immune. There is no safeguard. No chosen people. Poets suffer the scourge, so do parsons, taxidermists and taxi drivers; all-in wrestlers get it, so do all-in bargain hunters; the poor, the rich, dockers, and doctors . . . . Yes and even specialists in urology.

You find them all among the penny spenders.

Frequency is just one of those things. Irritating, painful, messy, seldom fatal, always inconvenient; nevertheless the affliction also can be a source of great amusement to one's friends. Nice people roar with laughter. Others smirk smugly and say to their wives 'Imagine having a trotting husband!'

Assuming you have been stricken with Frequency and your regular doc can't help, let me recommend that you go the full hog with specialists. You will enter an extraordinary new world that can also be amusing. Circumstances are unpleasant, but in a macabre way it is all very funny.

I don't like to spread panic, but someone must speak up for the underdog – especially when he stops at every lamp post.

George Houghton, *The Penny Spenders*

*Man passing water*

*Woman passing water*

**Etchings by Rembrandt**

A 66lb block of green ice fell into the garden of Mr and Mrs Chris Elkins, breaking three branches off a tree and denting the lawn.

'It gave me a bit of a shock,' Mr Elkins said. 'I was having a shave at the time when I heard a swishing noise followed by a thud.'

He and Mrs Elkins went into the garden and saw the ice.

'My wife wouldn't let me go near it, so I 'phoned the police. It certainly was a near miss. Another foot or so and it would have hit the house.'

Police took away the object for examination to their headquarters where it was identified as frozen urine.

A police spokesman said, 'When we found out what it was, we decided we would rather not have it lying around the station.' It has since melted away on the lawn outside the police station.

*Surrey Herald*, 10 September 1971

*Crossword solution (see p. 14).*

# ILL WIND
# (BLOW, WINDS, AND CRACK YOUR CHEEKS!)

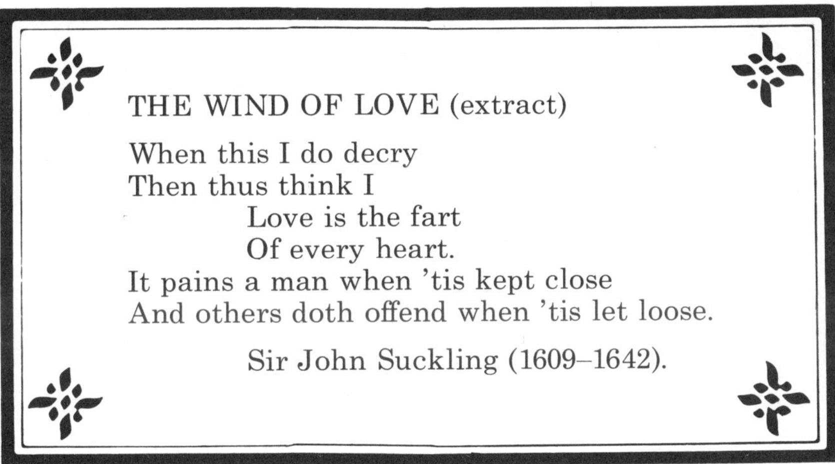
THE WIND OF LOVE (extract)

When this I do decry
Then thus think I
Love is the fart
Of every heart.
It pains a man when 'tis kept close
And others doth offend when 'tis let loose.

Sir John Suckling (1609–1642).

'Did you fart?'

'Of course I did! Do you think I always smell like this?

# Gas And Bloating

Gas is by far the most common digestive disturbance. Symptoms can be produced by either swallowed air, or gas formed by the action of putrefactive bacteria on various undigested foods in the intestines.

A bubble of air trapped in the stomach or in a loop of bowel can cause great distress. It causes distension of the viscera, thus stretching the nerve endings and causing pain, bloating and strange gurgling sounds. Those who eat rapidly and gulp their meals may trap air along with their food. Gum chewing, thumb sucking, poorly fitting dentures and so on, stimulate excessive production of saliva which must be swallowed – along with extra air.

If swallowed air does successfully pass the stomach, it may collect further down at the splenic or hepatic fixtures of the colon. The result is abdominal distress. It is the inability to remove normal or increased amounts of air which can lead to symptoms of gas.

Posture may also be important to the entrapment of air in the intestines. To obtain relief, take a stroll after meals, or try the following exercise. Lie on a flat surface. A bed is fine. Bring both knees up to your chest for a count of 10. Then try the knee-chest position while lying on your stomach. Doctors sometimes recommend heat, massage, or a gentle enema to relieve the condition. All of these methods have varying results.

From *Encyclopaedia of Common Diseases.*

Beans, beans,
Are good for the heart
The more you eat
The more you fart
The more you fart
The better you feel
So let's have beans
For every meal

# BEANZ MEANZ FARTZ

*OUTRAGED HOST (TO GUEST WHO HAS INADVERTENTLY PERPETRATED AN EMBARRASSING HISTRIONIC EFFECT):*

"Dammit man, you've just farted in front of my wife".

*DEFAULTING GUEST (NONCHALANTLY):*

"I do apologise, my dear fellow I didn't realise it was her turn"

# God put the smell in farts for those who are hard of hearing

*Methane from the anaerobic fermentation of organic matter in the absence of oxygen*
A chicken produces $\frac{1}{2}$ cubic foot of gas per day equal to 300 BTU (British Thermal Units).
A man produces 1 cubic foot of gas a day equivalent to 600 BTU.
A cow produces 8 cubic feet of gas a day equivalent to 4800 BTU.
A pig produces 9 cubic feet of gas a day equivalent to 5400 BTU or enough to boil 5 kettles of water.

From *Self-Sufficiency* by John Seymour

A man comes home on his birthday to be greeted by his wife at the door. She blindfolds him, leads him into the drawing-room and there tells him that she has three surprises for him. She hands him two parcels and tells him that she will be right back.

The first he recognises by feel as a pipe, and opening the second he discovers what feels like a bath-robe. He sits patiently waiting for his wife, his new pipe in his mouth, and breaks wind noisily several times, fanning the smell away with his new dressing-gown.

His wife returns, takes off the blindfold to show him his third surprise; all his best friends are sitting silently around him in paper hats, waiting for the party to begin.

# Farting as an Art

Joseph Pujol (1857–1945), better known as Le Petomane, performed his extraordinary act in Paris, at the Moulin Rouge, in the 1890s. At the height of his career he was grossing more at the box-office than Sarah Bernhardt.

His particular attraction was that he could inhale air through his anus and then, by controlling his abdominal and rectal muscles, produce musical notes which varied in intensity and timbre from the sound of the violin and bass to that of the trombone. Apart from farting recognisable tunes, he could sustain one note for anything up to fifteen seconds. His audiences, which sometimes included royalty, were reputed to cry with convulsive laughter, and many fainted, although not through asphyxiation; his farts were said to be completely odourless.

By squatting in a basin of water he was also able to fill his large intestine, retain the liquid for some time and then, by standing and leaning forward, could project the water some five metres in one single jet. Another property of this remarkable anus was that, such was the force of air from it, Le Petomane was able to blow out a candle placed one foot away. He was billed as 'the only artist who pays no author's royalties'.

An experiment seen through the eyes of James Gilray

He cogheth first, and knokketh therwithal
Upon the wyndowe, right as he dide er.
    This Alison answerde, 'Who is ther
That knokketh so? I warante it a theef.'
    'Why, nay,' quod he, 'God woot, my sweete leef,
I am thyn Absolon, my deerelyng.
Of gold,' quod he, 'I have thee broght a ryng.
My mooder yaf it me, so God me save;
Ful fyn it is, and thereto wel ygrave
This wol I yeve thee, if thou me kisse.'
    This Nicholas was risen for to pisse,
And thoughte he wolde amenden al the jape;
He sholde kisse his ers er that he scape.
And up the wyndowe dide he hastily,
And out his ers he putteth pryvely
Over the buttok, to the haunch-bon;
And therewith spak this clerk, this Absolon,
'Spek, sweete bryd, I noot nat where thou art.'
    This Nicholas anon leet fle a fart,
As greet as it had been a thonder-dent,
That with the strook he was almost yblent;
And he was redy with his iren hoot,
And Nicholas amydde the ers he smoot.

Geoffrey Chaucer, *The Miller's Tale.*

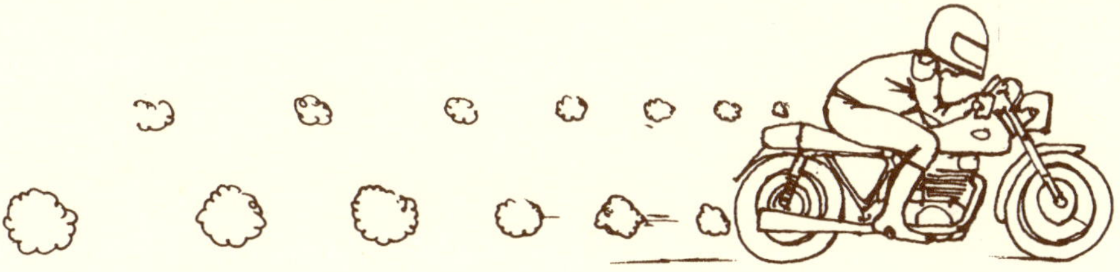

Did you know that if it weren't for the non-polarity of carbon-carbon and carbon-hydrogen bonds, you'd dissolve yourself when you farted in the bath?

Letter in *Bike* magazine.

Long life to all you dear ones, Papa and my Mamma,
My sister and her brother! Hey sassa! Houp sassa!
And Woferl too and also the mistress of his heart.
And this for evermore, my dears, as long as he can fart,
As long as he can piddle and shit it with the best,
So long will he and Rosie and Nan and all be blest—
A charming crew! Alas, to bed I now must creep,
For I hear it stricking midnight, when we all should be asleep.

**Wolfgang Amadeus Mozart**. *Letter to his father, Leopold, 20 December 1777.*

*Clown.* Are these, I pray you, wind-instruments?
*1st Musician.* Ay, marry, are they, sir.
*Clown.* O, thereby hangs a tail.
*1st Musician.* Whereby hangs a tale, sir?
*Clown.* Marry, sir, by many a wind instrument
that I know.

William Shakespeare, *Othello*, Act III scene I

**Blue Streak**

Daddy used to break wind for us and light the result with a match. It looked like a gas flame and we christened it 'Blue Streak'.

(Daughter of a British Knight.)

The honeymoon is over when the husband farts in bed

Aubrey Beardsley, from 'Lysistrata'.

MUSICAL BUMPS

BEETHOVEN FIFTH SYMPHONY

The Longest Known Scatological Palindrome
T. Eliot, top bard, notes putrid tang emanating. Is sad!
I'd assign it a name: 'gnat-dirt, upset on drab pot toilet.'

A man in an hotel breaks wind in the bath. A few minutes later a bellboy knocks on the door and comes in with a bottle of beer on a tray.

'I didn't order a beer.'

'I distinctly heard you, sir, say 'Hey bub, bring up a bottle of Budweiser.'

The honeymoon really is over when the husband farts in bed, shouts, 'Burglars!' and his wife dives under the sheets.

# BUMF

# (PAPERING OVER THE CRACKS)

I have, answered Gargantua, by a long and curious experience, found out a means to wipe my bum, the most lordly, the most excellent, and the most convenient that ever was seen. Once I did wipe me with a gentlewoman's velvet mask, another time with a lady's neckerchief, and after that I wiped me with some earpieces of hers made of crimson satin . . . with a page's cap, garnished with a feather after the Switzer's fashion . . . a March-cat, . . . my mother's gloves . . . with sage, with fennel, with anet, with marjoram, with roses, with gourd-leaves, with beets, with colewort, with vine-leaves, with mallows, wool-blade, with lettuce, with spinach-leaves . . . then I wiped my tail in the sheets, in the coverlet, in the curtains, with a cushion, with an arras hanger, with a green carpet, with a table cloth, with a napkin, with handkerchief, with a combing cloth, with a pillow, with a pantoufle, with a ponch, with a pannier . . . then with a hat . . . afterwards I wiped my tail with a hen, with a cock, with a pullet, with a calf's skin, with a hare, with a pigeon, with a cormorant, with an attorney's leg, with a montero, with a coif, with a falconer's lure. But to conclude, I say and maintain, that of all the torcheculs, arsewipes, bumfodders, tail napkins, bung-hole cleaners, and wipe-breeches, there is none ever in the world comparable to the neck of a goose, that is well downed, if you hold her neck betwixt your legs.

François Rabelais, *Gargantua.*

A Handy Hint . . .

**When the leaves on a roll of soft toilet tissue become separated and uneven with the attendant dangers of a finger slipping thru' – unroll the *top* layer only until, magically, the perforations line up.**

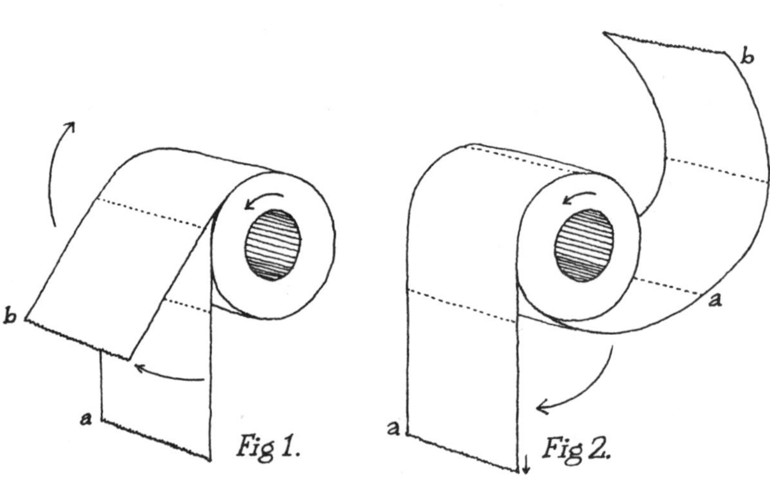


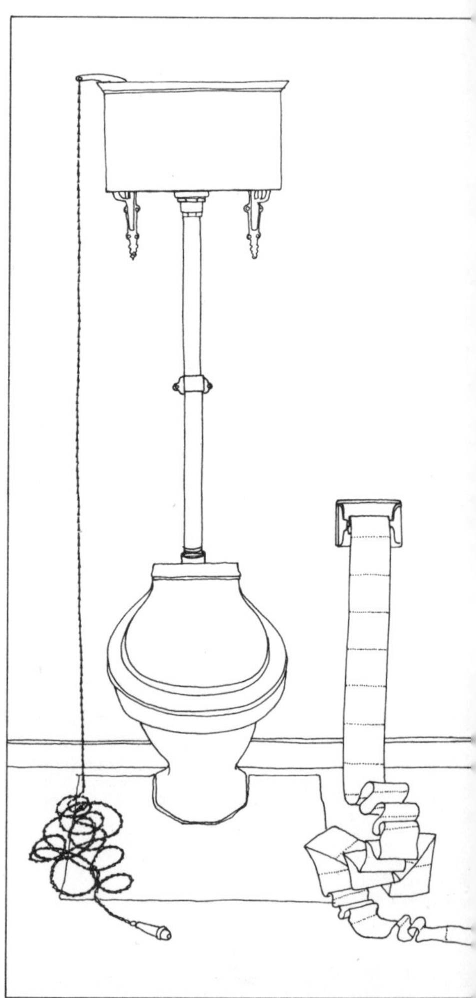

The débutante and her boy-friend were necking on the chaise-longue in the drawing-room, long after midnight.

'Sorry, old girl,' announced Percy, 'but I'm just bursting to go to the loo.'

'Well, don't go to the bathroom,' hissed Charlotte. 'You'll wake Mummy and Daddy, and I told them you've gone home.'

'Oh, right-ho,' sniggered the deb's delight, 'I'll go in the garden.'

'No, that's no good. It's right under their window, and they'll hear the splashing. Go in the kitchen sink.'

Percy made it to the kitchen, and within five minutes he hobbled back.

'I say,' he enquired plaintively. 'Got any paper?'

'What is the life, or how long will the average mail order catalogue last, in just the plain ordinary eight family three holer?' It stumped me for a spell, but this being a reasonable question I checked up, and found that by placin' the catalogue in there, say in January – when you get a new one – you should be into the harness section by June; but of course, that ain't through apple-time, and not countin' on too many city visitors, either. An' another thing – they've been puttin' so many of those stiff-colored sheets in the catalogue here lately that it makes it hard to figger. Something really ought to be done about this and I've thought about takin' it up with Mr Sears Roebuck hisself.'

Charles Sale, *The Specialist*.

While shepherds watched their flocks by night,
All shitting on the ground,
An angel of the Lord came down
And handed paper round.

If perchance there is no paper
Underneath you'll find a scraper;
If the scraper can't be found
Wipe your arse along the ground.

Faced with the sticky problem of how to introduce soft toilet tissue to traditional 'hard' liners, salesmen chose this method:
Squeeze a large dollop of mustard onto a tea-tray, wipe first with traditional non-absorbent hard tissue, then perform the same exercise using the soft brand – hey presto! a clean tray.

A farmer once telephoned Sears Roebuck and Company to ask the price of toilet paper. He was told to look at page 330 of their catalogue.
'If I had your catalogue,' he said, 'would I be asking the price of toilet paper?'

The average British family uses 90 rolls of lavatory paper every year, equivalent to roughly two miles and a total cost of some £9.

*Which* magazine.

Her Majesty's Stationery office issues 2,000,000 rolls of 'hard' paper to the Civil Service and Armed Forces each year. This represents two thousand million sheets or 180,000 miles: not quite enough to reach the moon.
Going 'soft' would cost the British taxpayer an estimated £½m. more per annum.

HM Stationery Office

It is not necessary to wipe the anus with three pebbles or three pieces of cloth; one pebble or one piece of cloth will suffice. However, if one wipes oneself with a bone or a sacred object, such as a piece of paper with the name of God on it, one should not say one's prayers in this state.

Ayatollah Khomeiny, *Principles*

In Victorian times toilet rolls were obtained without embarrassment, by being purchased under the verbal disguise of 'curl papers'; such were its advantages that the lady of the house managed to conquer her blushes at the store.

In 1879 two Philadelphia brothers called Irvin and Clarence Scott had started a business to sell wrapping paper, and seeing a growing market in toilet papers they overcame the problem of marketing a product which did not exist officially in polite society, by making rolls which merchants could sell discreetly under their own brand names. It was in 1899 that the Scott brothers began marketing their own national brand, called Waldorf.

I had just finished in the public WC and was slipping my braces back over my shoulders and reaching for my jacket from the hook on the back of the door. At first I hardly heard the voice from the next cubicle, it was so very muted, but finally I made out the worried plea: 'I say, I'm terribly sorry to bother you, but I've just finished, and there isn't any paper here. Could you possibly pass a few sheets under the wall?'

I had myself just used the last of the bumf in my own closet. 'None here, old man,' I replied sympathetically. 'Afraid I used the last myself.'

There was a strained silence, then:

'Got an evening paper?'

'Dear me, no I haven't. It's delivered to my home.'

Another agonised pause:

'Got any old letters you don't need?'

'No, I deal with all that sort of stuff at the office.'

'Stamps . . .' muttered the voice hoarsely. 'Got a few stamps in your wallet?'

I was mortified. 'Look, I really am frightfully sorry, but no . . . I haven't.'

The final silence was so long that it clearly heralded a decision of some consequence.

'Look,' said the voice in desperation, 'can you possibly change two fivers for a ten?'

I knew a gentleman, who was so good a manager of his time, that he would not even lose that small portion of it which the calls of nature obliged him to pass in the necessary-house, but gradually went through all the Latin poets in those moments. He bought, for example, a common edition of Horace, of which he tore off gradually a couple of pages, carried them with him to that necessary place, read them first, and then sent them down as a sacrifice to Cloacina; this was so much time fairly gained; and I recommend to you to follow his example. It is better than only doing what you cannot help doing at those moments; and it will make any book which you shall read in that manner, very present to your mind.

Lord Chesterfield, Letter to his son 11 December 1747

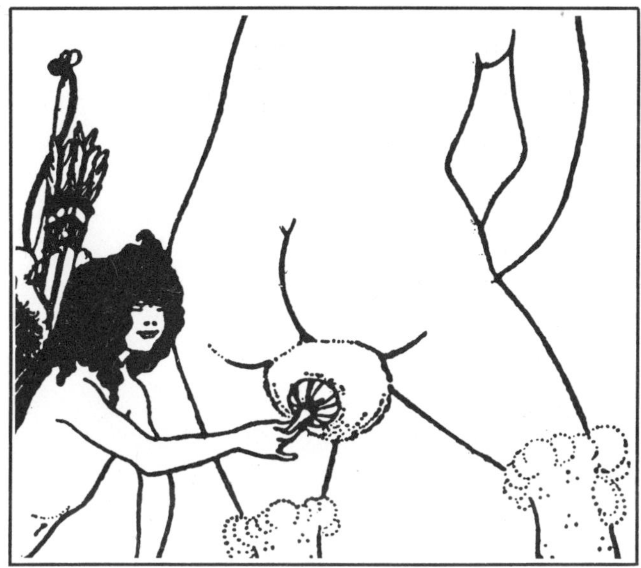

*Detail from 'Lysistrata' by Aubrey Beardsley*

I was on a tour in Bradford. The landlady there, Mrs Berol, always greeted me with open arms. This visit the whole family was gathered for a welcoming ham tea. I arrived, late off the train, taken very short indeed, and had to go through the torture of kisses and hugs and 'How *are* you, Mr R?', 'Don't ee look *well*, Muriel', and ''Ow *was* the trip, Mr R?' As soon as was decent I got Mrs Berol's ear and whispered my plight.

'Oh,' she said, in a polite vocal tone, ''ang *on* everybody, Mr R's been taken a bit short. Off you go Mr R . . . You know, through the parlour and out the back . . . Oh, and Muriel . . . give Mr R the wrapper off the new loaf.'

North Country comedian.

Feb. 28. The Frost severer than ever in the night as it even froze the Chamber Pots under the Beds.

The Rev. James Woodforde, *Diary of a Country Parson* (1785)

# HARD UP

## (DEAD PAN)

a laxative which preserves his normal good-humour instead of making him surly and out-of-sorts. What a pity he doesn't take Lixen! For Lixen is thorough without being harsh. Non-griping and non-habit-forming, it is so completely *natural* that children, adults and invalids can take it with equal confidence and safety. From chemists only. LIXEN LOZENGES (fruit-flavoured) 8½d. & 1/2. LIXEN ELIXIR (in bottles) 1/2, 2/-, 3/6.

MADE BY ALLEN & HANBURYS LTD., LONDON, E.C.3.

THE *good-natured* LAXATIVE

A man went into an optician, carrying a magnificent polished rosewood box, about three foot long, beautifully inlaid with ivory. He went up to the assistant at the counter and opened the box. It was lined with green baize and contained an enormous turd, about two and a half feet long and nine inches in circumference.

'Good grief,' said the assistant. 'Did you do this?'

'Yes,' said the man simply.

'But you don't want an optician, you need to go and see a doctor.'

'No,' said the man, 'it's you I need. Every time I do one, my eyes water.'

My mother had a positive mania for regular bowel movements which she said was the basis of all good health, and the doctor did nothing to discourage her by constantly asking to see my tongue on his rare visits. This merely served to confirm her aberration to purge me within an inch of my life. Even today I cannot view a bottle of syrup of figs without wanting to heave, and my stomach contracts with spasmodic horror in remembrance of the griping pains of yesteryear.

Lois Bourne, *Witch amongst Us*.

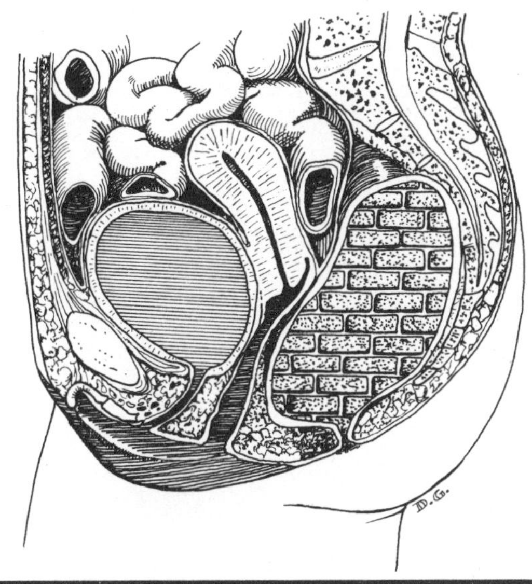

'Dr. A. Cabe of Lyons, France, writes that he had in his practice a very obstinate case of constipation in a female subject 80 years of age, who for 60 years had suffered in consequence of a severe attack of dysentery encountered in her youth. The patient having had no passage for 40 days, the doctor tried to induce a contraction of the intestines by the application of electricity. He inserted the negative pole of a Gaiffe battery into the rectum and applied the positive to the navel, and in the course of two minutes the results were completely satisfactory.'

August 1870

Regularity of habits is also important. It's a good idea to regulate your bowel habits for the same time every day. A good time for this might be after eating a hearty breakfast which includes fresh or stewed fruit, and unrefined cereal product such as granola, wheat germ, or oatmeal, and some whole grain bread products. If that's too much cereal and bread, replace some of it with a few teaspoons of unprocessed bran.

Once in the bathroom, try to relax. Pick up a magazine or a book. Just make sure you aren't reading about constipation, because the idea is to take your mind off what you are doing. Stay put for about ten minutes, regardless of what happens. Repeat daily. Eventually, your colon will get the idea.

Speaking of toilets, it has been said that toilet bowls themselves cause problems by being too high. Critics say that feet should be planted firmly upon the ground to induce a proper bowel movement, and that toilets today tend to be too high. So if you want to, put a stack of old books under each foot, or keep a footstool nearby.

*Encyclopaedia of Common Diseases*

Opinions differ enormously on what is considered to be the perfect stool, and how to achieve it, as demonstrated here in two conflicting views on the efficacy of bran:

## (1) FOR

**The idea that bran can abolish constipation is far from new. But until recently, it had more of the status of a folk remedy than of a medically-approved treatment. Its present wide acceptance as an unconstipating food can probably be attributed mostly to Surgeon Captain Thomas L. Cleave of the British Royal Navy.**

**Here is part of a letter published in the *Lancet* in 1962, from Dr Harold Dodd: 'Constipation is an ailment of so-called civilization and it can be greatly relieved by the way we live. . . . I cannot speak too highly of Surgeon Captain Cleave's prescription – one tablespoon of unprocessed bran daily. It restores to the diet what the miller has taken out. For several years I have practiced and prescribed a dessertspoon of unprocessed bran and one of unprocessed wheat germ daily. It is moistened according to taste with milk, gravy, soup, coffee, or fruit juice. In most patients it insures a daily formed stool as smooth as with liquid paraffin.'**

***Encyclopaedia of Common Diseases.***

## (2) AGAINST

**The 'roughage' idea for regulating the bowels is a real curse. 'Roughage' has given rise to many digestive diseases (duodenitis, enteritis and colitis leading to duodenal ulcer and ulcerated bowels being some of the more serious of those diseases); but it has never yet cured one of them or cured any of the *causes* of constipation.**

**How did this 'roughage' idea start? It began as a catchword to launch a successful campaign of certain industrialists who wanted to dump their waste products on the market. The 'roughage' craze developed with the arrival of *bran* on the shop counters. So good was the publicity and advertising work on this new product, bran, that it soon found its way into health food stores and many recommended health food diets. You would doubtless fly to it as a superlative and safe article of 'food' and roughage. But my sincere advice to you is – *don't*! Avoid it like the proverbial plague.**

***Encyclopaedia of Digestive Disorders,* ed. Frank Roberts.**

Notwithstanding the above, it is now generally considered wise to add a proportion of roughage to the Western diet, to counteract the over-refinement in convenience (sic) foods.

*Bran Snaps:*

100gr. butter or margarine.
75gr. black treacle.
75gr. soft brown sugar.
100gr. rolled oats.
100gr. bran.

1. Melt butter, treacle and sugar together in a pan.
2. Stir in oats and bran, mixing well.
3. Spread mixture smoothly onto a baking tin.
4. Bake in moderate oven – 180°C/350°F for 30 minutes.

Leave for 5 minutes or so, then cut into squares, and eat when cool.
N.B. Cinnamon, Ginger or Nutmeg can be added.

Even if Napoleon made no mention of liver trouble the board ought to have investigated the possibility if they knew that he had been suffering severely during the Waterloo campaign from prolapsed piles. Piles were a cross which the Bonaparte family had to bear. Napoleon had written to Jerome recommending the application of leeches, which he said he had found very effective. This is an indication that his piles were no mere transient minor trouble. The first occasion on which Napoleon had had to resort to leeches was during his Italian campaign. His piles were probably associated with his tendency to chronic constipation; but the condition is sometimes due to trouble in the liver.

Frank Richardson, *Napoleon's Death: An Inquest*

Other desirable foods are fruit in general, but in particular raw apples, figs, and prunes; and vegetables, especially cabbage, tomatoes, and any containing a large residue. Honey, marmalade, treacle and porridge are all good. Spinach boiled to a pulp in its own moisture is a good, easily digested laxative, especially for elderly people, but only fresh spinach should be used. It can be mixed in almost any diet.

Some people when affected give themselves a powerful purge, usually one of a number of advertised patents. This is wrong, for this method is followed by an intense reaction on the bowels, causing further constipation, and a vicious circle is set up.

From *The Romany Way to Health.*

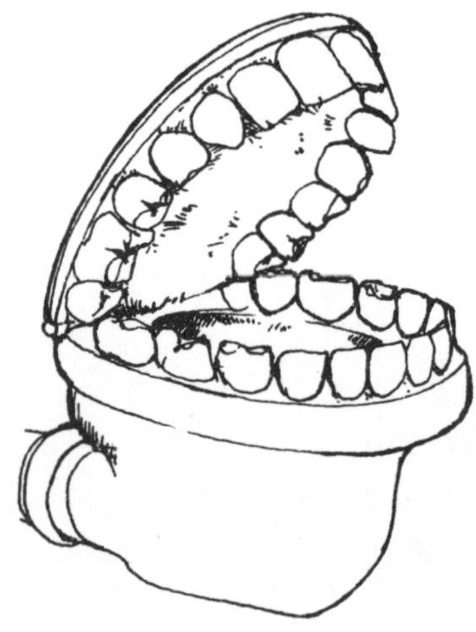

Extract from letter sent to the Pensions Office:
'Re your dental enquiry – the teeth on top are alright but the teeth in my bottom hurt terribly.'

# RUNNING AMUCK

## (THE LONELINESS OF THE LONG DISTANCE RUNNER)

'When did you first realize you were suffering from diarrhoea?'

'When I took off my cycle-clips'

A colonel went to a regimental dinner at which he ate and drank to excess – so much so that, on his way home, he was sick down the front of his mess (sic) jacket. When he reached his quarters, he told his batman: 'Comin' home from dinner some bounder was tight, blundered into me and puked down me mess jacket, the cad. You might clean it up, and remind me in the morning to give that man fourteen days in the guardhouse, will you?'

The following morning the batman returned his clothes cleaned and pressed. 'If I were you, sir, I'd make it twenty-eight days – the dirty devil shat in your trousers as well.'

## From *Portnoy's Complaint*, by Philip Roth

'Get in here, please, you,' says my mother. 'Why did you flush the toilet when I told you not to?'

'I forgot.'

'What was in there that you were so fast to flush it?'

'Diarrhea.'

'Was it mostly liquid or was it mostly poopie?'

'I don't look! I didn't look! Stop saying poopie to me – I'm in high school!'

'Oh, don't you shout at *me*, Alex. I'm not the one who gave you diarrhea, I assure you. If all you ate was what you were fed at home, you wouldn't be running to the bathroom fifty times a day. Hannah tells me what you're doing, so don't think I don't know.'

She's missed the underpants! *I've been caught!* Oh, *let* me be dead! I'd just as soon!

'Yeah, what do I do . . . ?'

'You go to Harold's Hot Dog and *Chazerai* Palace after school and you eat French fries with Melvin Weiner. Don't you? Don't lie to me either. Do you or do you not stuff yourself with French fries and ketchup on Hawthorne Avenue after school? Jack, come in here, I want you to hear this,' she calls to my father, now occupying the bathroom.

'Look, I'm trying to move my bowels,' he replies. 'Don't I have enough trouble as it is without people screaming at me when I'm trying to move my bowels?'

'You know what your son does after school, the *A* student, who his own mother can't say poopie to any more, he's such a *grown-up?* What do you think your grown-up son does when nobody is watching him?'

'Can I please be left alone, please?' cries my father. 'Can I have a little peace, please, so I can get something accomplished in here?'

'Just wait till your father hears what you do, in defiance of every health habit there could possibly be. Alex, answer me something. You're so smart, you know all the answers now, answer me this: how do you think Melvin Weiner gave himself colitis? Why has that child spent half his life in hospitals?'

'Because he eats *chazerai*.'

'Don't you dare make fun of me!'

'All right,' I scream, 'how *did* he get colitis?'

'Because he eats *chazerai!* But it's not a joke! Because to him a meal is an O Henry bar washed down by a bottle of Pepsi. Because his breakfast consists of, do you know what? The most important meal of the day – not according just to your mother, Alex, but according to the highest nutritionists – and do you know what that child eats?'

'A doughnut.'

'A doughnut is right, Mr Smart Guy, Mr Adult. And *coffee*. Coffee and a doughnut, and on this a thirteen-year-old *pisher* with half a stomach is supposed

to start a day. But you, thank God, have been brought up differently. You don't have a mother who gallavants all over town like some names I could name, from Bam's to Hahne's to Kresge's all day long. Alex, tell me, so it's not a mystery, or maybe I'm just stupid – only tell me, what are you trying to do, what are you trying to prove, that you should stuff yourself with such junk when you could come home to a poppyseed cookie and a nice glass of milk? I want the truth from you. I wouldn't tell your father,' she says, her voice dropping significantly, 'but I *must* have the truth from you.' Pause. Also significant. 'Is it just French fries, darling, or is it more? . . . Tell me, please, what other kind of garbage you're putting into your mouth so we can get to the bottom of this diarrhea! I want a straight answer from you, Alex. Are you eating hamburgers out? Answer me, please, is that why you flushed the toilet – was there hamburger in it?'

'I told you – I don't look in the bowl when I flush it! I'm not interested like you are in other people's poopie!'

It was very late one night in the club, and the General and the Admiral, both very old, were remembering the good days of the past.

'Once went tiger huntin' in Poona,' said the General. 'Now that's a man's work. Cuttin' yer way through the jungle. Chatterin' monkeys, parrots in the treetops, and suddenly, without warning, a huge tiger sprang out of the undergrowth straight at me, and went "**YAHAGGERRAH!!!**" – I shat meself.'

'Not surprised,' said the Admiral, 'tiger coming at you like that.'

'No,' said the General. 'Not *then* . . . just now, when I went "**YAHAGGERRAH!**"'

## A CASE HISTORY

A relatively mild and simple illustrative case is that of a prominent businessman who stated at the first consultation that he was in perfect health but wished to discuss a rather absurd thing that was happening to him during the last three months. With much embarrassment he explained that he had been forced to give up golf, of which he was very fond. The reason for this decision was the fact that every time he approached the fifth green he was assailed by violent and uncontrollable diarrhoea. When he was asked how all this had started, he looked taken aback and rather puzzled. After a little thought he declared that he could not remember the first time it had occurred. He then changed the subject and cheerfully explained that as long as he kept away from the golf course his stools were perfectly normal. Smiling, he commented, 'Idiotic, isn't it?' He was told that he could be cured only if he was able to remember all the circumstances surrounding the first time that he had had such an attack and was sent home to think about it.

The next day he returned and produced the following story in a less light-hearted mood. It had all started when one morning he had been dissatisfied with his evacuation and had casually swallowed one of his wife's pills which he found in the bathroom cupboard. In the midst of a very busy morning in his office, a lady of his acquaintance had telephoned to ask him if he cared to join her in a golf match in the afternoon. He had felt flattered and had readily accepted. The little pill swallowed in the bathroom had been forgotten, until suddenly it began to take effect at the approach to the fifth green. In a flurry of embarrassment he had made some silly excuse and dashed away to crouch behind a clump of bushes. When he returned to the game, his high-spirited companion had kept up a string of merry references to his vanishing act during the rest of the match. He now remembered that her frivolous remarks had needled him to the core, though he could not recollect her actual words.

Two days later he had played a round with a business friend and was again forced to beat an undignified retreat from the fifth green. He had returned to his friend saying that his lunch had not agreed with him and that he had been sick. He had abandoned the game and driven home. About ten days passed before he played again. He claimed to have forgotten the whole unpleasant incident until it happened again when he reached the fifth green. Now he was furious and decided to set about getting over this nonsense. In this he failed hopelessly and finally gave up playing. That was difficult because everyone knew that he was a keen golfer and explanations were demanded. He had sought plausible excuses and had been forced to invent fictitious board meetings, a sprained ankle, a threatening cold and the like. Occasionally he had been tempted to accept an invitation to play,

but then he had felt an increasing urge to go to stool, which vanished as soon as he cancelled the appointment.

In this case the first attack of diarrhoea was caused by a laxative and was therefore not psychosomatic. But all subsequent attacks were due to the panic evoked by the repressed memory of the first incident and its devastating effect upon his modesty and his pride. As soon as this mechanism was explained and accepted, he was advised to play another golf course a few miles away in a different town and then to play a single round on his usual course and report. Nothing happened on either occasion, and he was able to resume his matches as before.

Dr A.T.W. Simeon, *Man's Presumptuous Brain.*

Two men in a pub.

*1st Man:* Phew, you smell as if you've filled your trousers.
*2nd Man:* I have.
*1st Man:* Why the hell don't you go to the Gents and clean yourself up a bit?
*2nd Man:* Because I haven't finished yet.

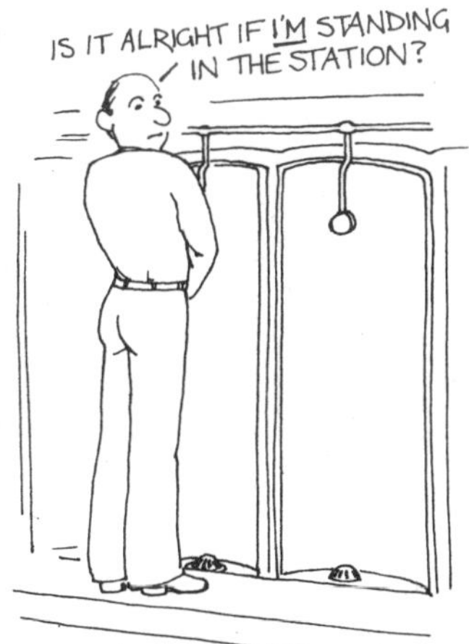


In the early '50s one of the musicians in a big band was hurrying to catch a train for a gig up North. He had been delayed when he called off at a men's outfitters, to pick up a pair of trousers he had bought but which had needed alteration.

He made Euston station in time for the train, but just before he boarded he broke wind, to avoid embarrassment to himself and fellow travellers in the carriage. It proved to be a mistake. His stomach wasn't in the best of conditions, and instead of a relatively harmless pump he fouled his trousers grotesquely. There was nothing for it but to get on the train, lock himself in the lavatory, and repair the damage during the journey.

His underpants and trousers were in a really fearful state, quite past saving, and so, blessing his visit to the tailors, he bundled both into a nasty ball and heaved them out of the window as soon as the train was a decent distance from the station. Then, having cleaned himself up at the wash-basin, he turned to open his carrier – finding, to his dismay, only two brand new shirts.

YOU'RE PISSING ON YOUR SHOES ↑
PLEASE DON'T PUT FAG-ENDS DOWN THE LOO — IT MAKES THEM SOGGY AND DIFFICULT TO LIGHT
A LIGHT TO L
I DRINK THEREFORE I AM — I'M DRUNK THEREFORE I WAS
LOOK UP↑
T.S. ELIOT IS AN ANAGRAM OF TOILETS
TO BE OR NOT TO BE — SHAKESPE
To do is to be — ROUSSEAU
TO BE IS TO DO — SARTRE
Dobedobedobedo — SINATRA
LOOK UP↑
Some come here to read and write
Some come here to wonder
Some come here have a shit
And fart away like thunder
IS A LOO A RENDEZVOUS FOR QUEERS MY DEARS
DON'T LOOK AT
ON THE WALL
LOOK AT THE JO
A MAN'S AMBITION MUST BE SMALL WHO WRITES UPON THE SHITHOUSE WALL
STAND CL
YOU'RE FL
FLUSH HARD IT'S A LONG WAY TO THE KITCHEN
LOOK UP↑
Please shit in
We aim to please
Your aim would help

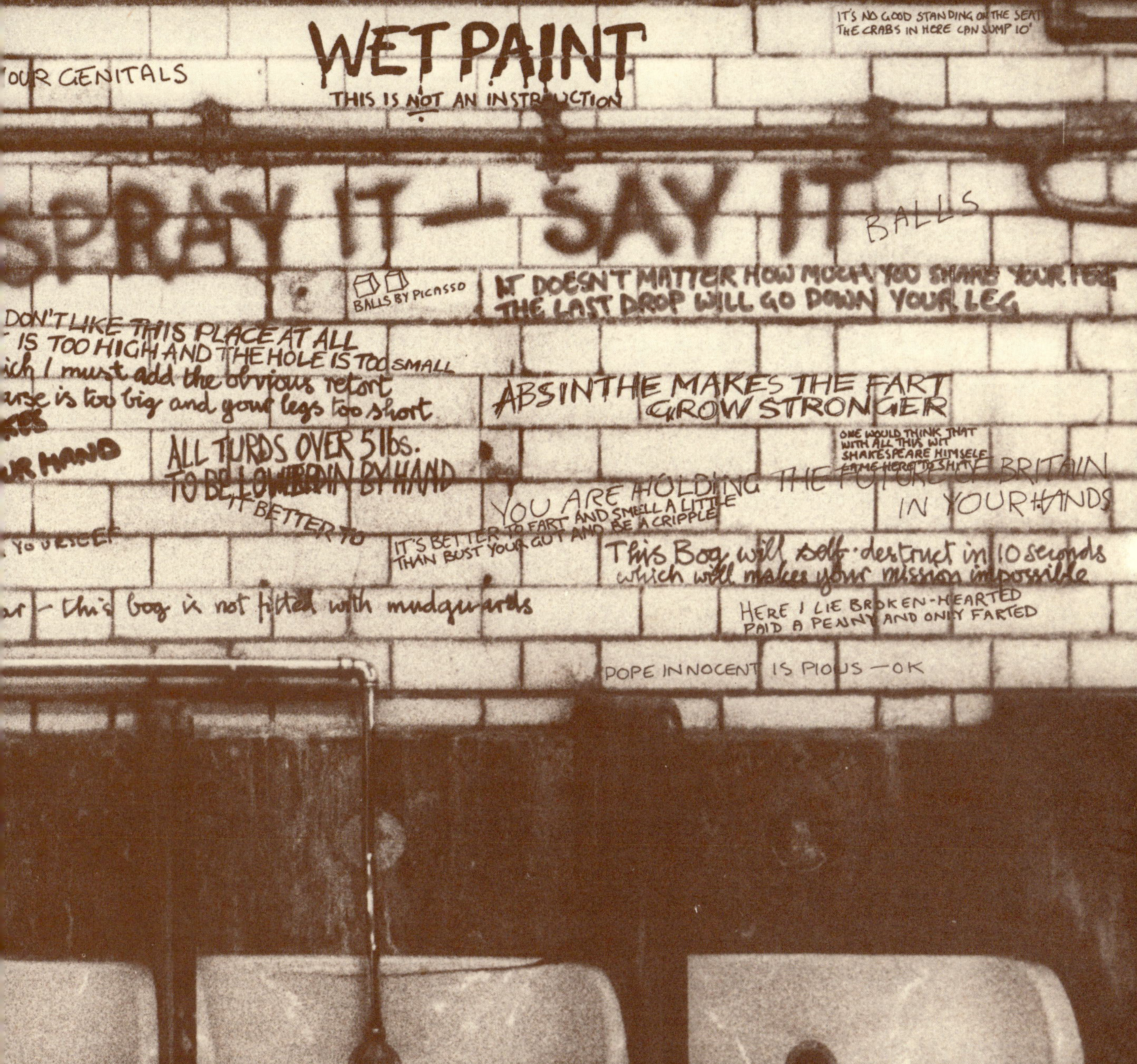

WET PAINT
THIS IS NOT AN INSTRUCTION
IT'S NO GOOD STANDING ON THE SEAT
THE CRABS IN HERE CAN JUMP 10'
OUR GENITALS
SPRAY IT — SAY IT
BALLS
BALLS BY PICASSO
IT DOESN'T MATTER HOW MUCH YOU SHAKE YOUR PEG
THE LAST DROP WILL GO DOWN YOUR LEG
DON'T LIKE THIS PLACE AT ALL
IS TOO HIGH AND THE HOLE IS TOO SMALL
ich I must add the obvious retort
urse is too big and your legs too short
ABSINTHE MAKES THE FART
GROW STRONGER
ALL TURDS OVER 5lbs.
ONE WOULD THINK THAT
WITH ALL THIS WIT
SHAKESPEARE HIMSELF
YOU ARE HOLDING THE FUTURE OF BRITAIN
IN YOUR HANDS
IT'S BETTER TO FART AND SMELL A LITTLE
THAN BUST YOUR GUT AND BE A CRIPPLE
This Bog will self-destruct in 10 seconds
which will makes your mission impossible
- this bog is not fitted with mudguards
HERE I LIE BROKEN-HEARTED
PAID A PENNY AND ONLY FARTED
POPE INNOCENT IS PIOUS — OK

**In these days of washing machines and disposable diapers it is hard to imagine the work involved in keeping baby clean two hundred years ago. One wonders how often it was properly done, as advised by *The Midwives' Book or the whole Art of Midwifery* in 1671:**

> . . . roul it up with soft cloths and lay it in the cradle: but in the swaddling of it be sure that all parts be bound up in their due place and order gently without any crookedness or rugged foldings; for infants are tender twigs and as you use them, so they will grow straight or crooked . . . lay the arms right down by the sides, that they may grow right. When the Navel-string is cut off, . . . bind a piece of Cotton or Wool over it, . . . and if the child be weak after this, anoint the child's body over with oil of acorns, for that will comfort and strengthen it and keep away the cold . . . Carry it often in the arms, and dance it, to keep it from the rickets and other diseases.
>
> After four months let loose the arms but still roul the breast and belly and feet to keep out cold air for a year, till the child have gained more strength. Shift the child's clouts often, for the Piss and Dung . . .
>
> When the child is seven months old you may (if you please) wash the body of it twice a week with warm water till it be weaned . . .

One of the psychiatrists I [talked to] had a patient whose Nanny used to tie him to his pot with straps. Simon T was allowed two 'tries', separated by half an hour each, and then given a thorough smacking and Gregory powder. Perhaps the most unpleasant instance I found was of a Nanny who used to insert her finger, causing considerable pain, deep into her little boy's rectum, allege she could 'feel it there', and upbraid him for 'holding back on her'.

In England, until very recently (and still among a great many people I suspect), it was thought 'natural' to bring children up strictly in this sphere. It is not. Dozens of cultures are the reverse of ours. The Siriono of South America, for instance, never punish a child even if it urinates or defecates on its parents. The mother makes no effort to train the child till it can walk, and even then it is done with endless help and encouragement and no punishment.

Similarly we tend to dismiss its effects. Yet severe toilet training had (and has) a number of perfectly well attested results. The most obvious of these was demonstrated to me by a surprise appearance of its reverse. 'I think you're right,' said the quite elderly man I was talking to, 'we probably were made too anxious about the whole business. But, even now you know, the relief when you have achieved, finally, a really satisfactory evacuation is very great. I think the enormous pleasure one experiences at a good motion counterbalances the despair at an inadequate one, or the horror at none at all.'

From *The Rise and Fall of the British Nanny* by Jonathan Gathorne-Hardy.

# POOH CORNER

## (OH, DEAR, WHAT CAN THE MATTER BE?)

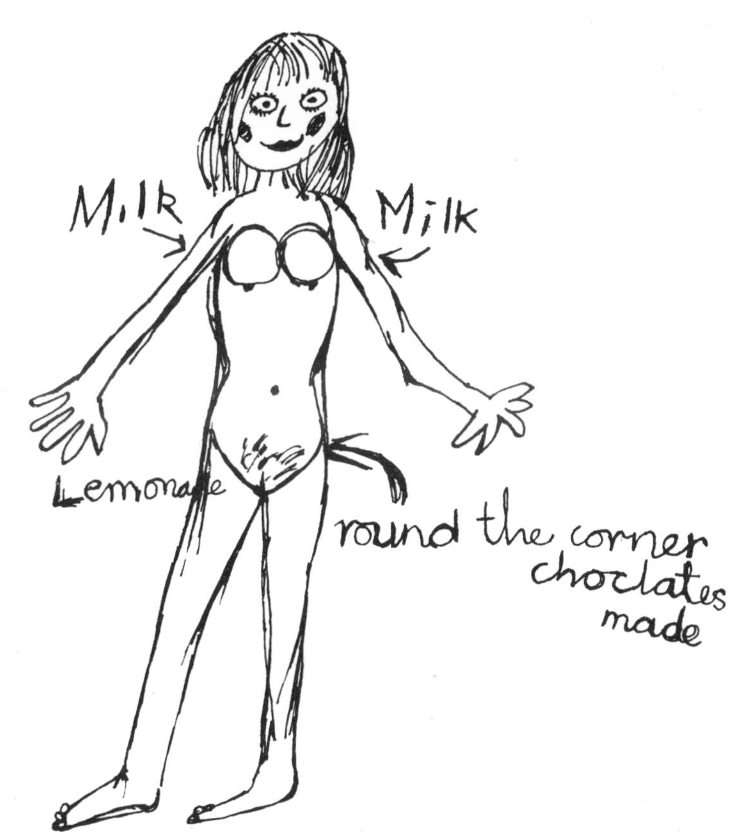

'Now,' said the teacher, 'today we're going to learn to use the word "definitely". Amanda, give me a sentence using the word correctly.'
'I'm definitely going to have peanut butter sandwiches for tea,' said Amanda.
'Wrong,' said the teacher. 'Not *definitely*. Your mother may not have any peanut butter in the house.'
Jennie tried next. 'Daddy is definitely going to take us out in the car this week-end.'
'No,' said the teacher. 'Not *definitely*. Your father's car might break down, or perhaps he might be called away on business.'
'Please Ma'am,' said Johnny. 'Do farts have lumps in them?'
'No,' said the teacher, 'they do not. Why?'
'Well, in that case, I've *definitely* shat myself!'

In some public schools, boys are given the privilege of a 'study' – either a room of their own, or one shared with two or three others – from the time that they enter the school. In others, studies either do not exist, or are only achieved towards the end of a boy's time at school. Public schools dislike privacy because they fear that it may encourage homosexuality. At my school, not only was it a crime to enter the dormitories during the day, but the lavatories had no doors. Defaecation was a public ritual performed after breakfast, with the next in the queue for one's lavatory seat observing the operation and urging one on to complete it as soon as possible. Some boys found this distasteful. The precautions taken to prevent boys ever being together in couples had the effect of making it equally difficult to be alone, except in special situations like the practice rooms of the Music School; and even those doors were furnished with spyholes.
From Anthony Storr's essay in *The World of the Public School*, ed. George Macdonald Fraser.

O here I sit in the peacefulness
Listening to the rippling piss
Now and then a fart is heard
Followed by a rumbling turd.

HERE I COME, What A CAPER,
Gotta pooh Got no paper,
Here comes my train, Musn't linger
Dash it all I'll use my Finger

Red white and blue
you dirty cockatoo
Sitting on the lamp post
Doing number two.

My old mans a dustman
He wears a dustmansHat
Farted through the Keyhole
And paralised the cat.

Hey diddle, diddle
The horse and cart
The cow did a piddle
The horse did a fart

In boarding school in New Zealand we used to lie very quiet in the dorm until someone yelled 'I've got one!' Then we'd all cluster round and watch, while he'd light it.
A 'greeny' wasn't any good, it was the 'blueys' you were after. You had to wear your pants, though, or the blow-backs could be terrible.

Antipodean property tycoon

CHICKEN SHIT?
As a boy in the West Indies we used to crap on the beach over the land crab holes. The trick was to get them before they got you, and the boy who hovered longest won the day.

Jamaican screenwriter

There was a little bunny
A-sitting on the dummy,
Eating bread and honey,
Waiting for his Mummy,
To come and wipe his bunny.

Me not worry,
Me not care,
Me do pooh pooh anywhere

Listen to Story 'bout a man named Ted
couldn't find a toilet so he went behind the shed.
Couldn't find the paper so he wiped it on the grass
And along came granny and shot him up the arse.

The night was dark and stormy,
The toilet light was dim,
I heard a splash and then a crash –
my God he's fallen in.

Rule Britannia
Britannia rule the seas;
Britons never never never shit green peas.

I'm in the army now
I tried to milk a cow
The cow farted and I departed
I'm in the airforce now.

Oh Dear what can the matter be?
Three old ladies locked in the lavatory
They were there from monday to saturday.
Nobody knew they where there.

Press The button
Pull the chain
Out comes a choo choo train.

In days of old
when knights were bold
And toilets weren't invented
They'd drop their load
in the middle of the road
And go off quite contented

I'm in the army now
I tried to milk a cow
I pulled its tail instead of its tit
And all I got was a bucket of shit.

Q. WHAT'S BROWN AND COMES STEAMING OUT OF COWS?
Answer. THE ISLE OF WIGHT FERRY.

'Imagine my shock then, when as a greying comic collector I dutifully plonked down my 7p for No. 1 of *Krazy* on the 16th of October 1976. I name the date with deliberation for it marks the breakthrough, or possibly soak-through, of kids' comedy into kids' comics. Everyone knows that children laugh more at lavatories than anything else, that it took a daring IPC editor to actually introduce toilet jokes into a comic. The strip was called ''Ello, it's cheeky'; the cartoonist was Frank McDiarmid.' Extract from '*How little Dennis spent the pennies*', an article by Dennis Gifford.

# ROYAL FLUSH
## (UPON THE THRONE)

Proclamation shall be made as well as in the Citie of London, as in other Cities, Boroughs and Townes, through the Realm of England, that all that do cast or throw any such annoyances, issues, dung, intrails or other ordure in Ditches, Rivers and Waters, he shall cause them to be removed . . . and carried away . . . upon pain to lose and forfeit to our Lord the King £20.

Part of a Proclamation issued by Richard II in 1388.

Of the transient here-today-and-gone-tomorrow smallest rooms with which modern science now meets human need, few could enjoy more adventitious glamour than those installed for a British coronation. All the world knows that one of the more impressive aspects of the ceremonial religious crowning of a monarch at Westminster is the time it takes. All the world wonders *how people manage*. Now I was one of the seven-thousand-odd carefully dressed and thoughtfully equipped (as to food and drink) guests commanded to attend the Abbey for the coronation of Queen Elizabeth II. Afterwards, the most persistent questions from the under-privileged, who saw so much more of the event than I did by staying at home and watching television, concerned the arrangements made to answer the calls of Nature, it being common knowledge that many of us were summoned at *6.30* a.m. and not released until early afternoon. I first encountered these arrangements when I was privileged to attend a dress rehearsal of the ceremony and, fighting back *folie de grandeur*, was assigned to the crimson chair to be occupied on the great day by a duchess. It was, in short, one of the best positions; but the illusion of scarlet and ermine did not entirely assuage human frailty – or curiosity. Upon my making known my need, I was ushered into the twilight by superbly clad officials with all the indulgent concern flaunted upon a spoilt child. When at length I found it, this smallest room, I realized that I had travelled east to the very steps of the altar. There, made fast by the frailest of bolts, concealed by the tenderest of prefabricated walls, to a majestic surge of ceremonial music, I usurped a throne. There were two hundred and thirteen chemical closets in Westminster Abbey on that day, forming a veritable rally of smallest rooms within those stately walls. Before a former coronation, an exalted and notoriously practical royal lady had inspected one of such conveniences and pointed out, perhaps from memory of sad experience, a serious defect. The little thrones were right up against the wall, as they might be in any conventional smallest room. But how could a Personage encompassed with splendid layers of ceremonial clothing *manage*?

John Pudney, *The Smallest Room*.

**The automatic flushing system of a 'gent's at Totnes Guildhall in Devon will be stopped when the Queen visits the town on 27 June – so that the noise does not disturb the Royal party. It has also been suggested the guests should stand in a semi-circle – to hide the entrance.**

***Sunday Pictorial***

Lavatory Rolls

When he [Louis XIV] travelled from one of his houses to another he only took women with him in his coach – his mistresses, later on his daughters or great friends . . . These journeys, except for the prestige they gave, were a real torment to his companions . . . The ladies were expected to be merry, to eat a great deal (he hated people to refuse food) and to have no physical needs which would force them to leave the coach. If by any chance they were taken ill, fainted, or felt sick, they could expect no sympathy; on the contrary, disfavour set in. One of his closest friends, the Duchesse de Chevreuse, Colbert's daughter, went alone with him from Versailles to Fontainebleau, a journey which took about six hours. Hardly had they left Versailles when she was seized with a pressing and seemingly irresistible need to retire. She knew that there was nothing to be done, though every mile that went by increased her misery . . . Several times she nearly fainted, but she hung on and at last they arrived. Her brother-in-law, the Duc de Beauvilliers, was waiting in the courtyard to meet them and she hissed in his ear the state she was in, saying she would never be able to get as far as her own room. He hurried her to the chapel and mounted guard while she relieved herself there.

Nancy Mitford, *The Sun King.*

This is the biggest waste of water in the country by far – you spend half a pint and flush two gallons.
The Duke of Edinburgh

King Francis I of France visited one of his favourite court ladies when, unfortunately, she was entertaining another lover. In the best tradition, she hid the gallant behind a pile of green branches lying in the hearth.

When the king had performed his duties with the lady, he wanted to make water, and got out of bed. Finding no other place near at hand, he went to the hearth, and watered the poor lover just like a garden watering-can, from all sides, on his face, in his eyes, his nose, his mouth, everywhere; some even went down his throat. I leave you to imagine how the knight felt, because he did not dare move, and what patience and endurance he displayed! When he had finished, the king bade the lady good-bye, and left. She locked the door behind him and called the gallant into her bed to warm him, and had him put on a clean shirt, and all not without laughter, after their great alarm . . . .

Source: Pierre de Bowdeille, Seigneur
and Abbé de Brantôme.

'If I were not a prince I would be a plumber.'
H.R.H. The Prince of Wales, later Edward VII, recovering from typhoid, after which he persuaded Queen Victoria to update the sanitation at Windsor Castle.

# POT POURRI

## (FLASH IN THE PAN)

HAVE YOU SEEN THE LOOS AT THE HOTEL SPLENDIDE?
ALL BRAND SPANKING NEW PASTEL BLUE TILES WITH
MATCHING FITTINGS AND AN AUTOMATIC FLUSHING SYSTEM...

PLEASE, NOT WHILE I'M EATING

# YOUR STARS

Quite probably you are following some Eastern religion right now. Fascinated by other cultures and philosophies, and always trying something new, you can be relied on to provide the latest brown-rice diet or inside information on colonic irregation. Study Yoga, if you aren't already doing so. Don't impose your fads on others.

Oh dear, oh dear. Piles, constipation, pills,potions. Poor Pisces, your hyper-sensitive digestion is so often a legacy from inhibitions formed in childhood. Leave all that behind you. Don't let your bowels rule your day. 'Relax and no laxatives' should be your motto.

You probably feel you're above all this – but you're reading it anyway, and most likely in secret. Don't get too snooty, remember Hitler was an Aries and something of a coprophiliac, as Langer reveals in his book *The Mind of Adolf Hitler*. (You'll probably want to read that too.)

A lot of talk and no action – they don't call it 'bull'-shit for nothing. You're too busy gossiping to heed the call of nature, and so often end up with constipation or cystitis. Lead a more active life.

All things to all men, silver-tongued Gemini, you can 'crap with the crowd' at a football match or have a 'quiet time' at your maiden aunt's without feeling out of place. Given to feasting and fasting by turn, don't be surprised at the variety of what you produce.

You would clean up the Universe soiled by those you love, but are woefully unforgiving of strangers. Hate 'going' anywhere but in your own home. Wonderfully tolerant of animals.

If you don't crack it at your usual time your ego takes a dive. You feel a sense of failure and hate yourself and everyone else too. Be patient, and you'll be fine – don't push to the head of the queue, remember there are others waiting, and you're not King of the Karzie.

You would like to pretend yours doesn't smell at all. Hard luck, it does and so does everyone else's. All the scented sprays, joss-sticks, matches and disinfectants you rush out and buy can't change it.
Godliness is next to cleanliness as far as you are concerned, and you will insist on a private bathroom and loo all to yourself, with a combination lock, if you possibly can.

A lover of beauty, you thrive in pretty surroundings either outside or in. A genuine antique water-closet will bring out the best in you. Don't worry too much about 'looking after yourself' in old age – there will always be someone there to help out.

The most basic and least 'hung-up' of all the signs, you have to be careful not to go too far over the top and let things get out of hand. Remember the sting in your tail – if anyone has left a mark on the pan it's probably you.

Far happier squatting behind an olive tree than sitting on the lavatory, you hate being closeted anywhere for too long and your movements are unpredictable. You tend to be shyer with your friends than with strangers. Take care not to put your foot in it.

You don't care if the loo is clean as long as it's royal. Your aim is high and you will probably go far.

A murderous witch's spell was that of obtaining some urine of the enemy, and then to buy a hen's egg without haggling over the price. Then on a Tuesday or a Saturday night the egg was taken into a field. A hole was made in its broad end and the white poured out, leaving the yolk. The egg was then filled with the urine while calling out the name of the enemy, and then sealed with a piece of wet unused parchment. Next, the egg was buried and the operator returned home without once looking back. As the egg decayed, the victim was attacked by jaundice. There was no cure unless the egg was withdrawn by the one who had buried it. If this was not done the victim died within a year.

Charles Bowness, *The Witch's Gospel*

There was a young Scot named McBride,
Who fell down a closet and died.
This man had a brother
Who fell down another,
And now they're interred side by side.

TRYING TO SQUEEZE A FART INTO A PINT POT

**If you stretch transparent cling film over the bowl and under the seat, you can cause an awful lot of trouble.**

**RAF base.**

—ACTING DUTY OFFICER—COMMERCIAL RADIO—

I was doing the early morning rounds just before one of c top DJ's was due to start in the studio, and as I pushed op the door of the Gents I noticed the most awful smell – rea ghastly – and I wondered what on earth it could be, so I we in to investigate.

As my eyes drew level with the edge of one of the s down toilets, I saw it. A huge torpedo, it was amazing, never seen anything like it, it was practically winking at m it wasn't human, I just couldn't believe any person cou have done it.

By now the DJ had arrived and I knew he'd be intereste so I rushed into the studio and told him about it. Of course wanted to see for himself, so he put on an extra long di and accompanied me. It was still there – awful – I swear was quivering. He was awestruck, he just stared, then said: 'I'll give you £500 if you'll dare to fish it out and bring to me in the studio while we're on the air,' and dashed ba just in time for the next announcement.

Well, it was winter, and my brown leather gloves look ju like a turd when they're twisted up, so I wet them slightly for a bit of glisten – and twisted them into a big roll, and lay on toilet paper in my hands . . . it needed three sheets. Th I crept into the studio. He was in the middle of a announcement and all hell broke loose. It's always hard tell when he's fooling about, but I'm sure the listeners mu have known something was really up; we practically had scrape him off the wall.

(N.B. When I asked the teller of this story why he hadn worn the gloves, presented the real thing, and thus won th £500, his grave answer was: 'You didn't see it. You didn see it.')

Q. What is the difference between a rich man and a poor man?

A. The rich man has a canopy over his bed, and the poor man has a can o' pee under his bed.

I am always amazed at the number of brown marks on clients' underpants. The British are by far the worst. I guess they think washing their bum is beneath them.

*Lady physiotherapist from New Zealand*

## Skipping Song

Wipe your bum from front to back
Don't leave clinkers in the crack
Wash your hands when you have been
Leave the lav fit for the Queen

'Wanted: A dog that neither barks nor bites,
Eats broken glass and shits diamonds.'
GOETHE

You know, people seem to regard death as an indictable crime. They are shocked if you mention it. I wait for it now without rancour or surprise. Every morning my valet tiptoes into my rooms as though he expects to find me dead in bed – but death, like constipation, is one of the commonplaces of human existence: Why shy away from it?

Somerset Maugham.